TESTIMONIALS FF
CONSULTIN

MW01050741

I have found Bill's passion for innovatio.., ...p.....d w.... ..... w..... experience; his commitment to team building with objectives; his capability as a facilitator without independent personal objectives; and his breadth of experience, not only as a consultant, but as one who has had to meet the payroll, combine to make Bill a unique and highly capable individual. Bill's leadership and commitment to team dynamics are invaluable. We utilized his innovative skills as a facilitator in leading complex groups of high-profile businesspersons to shared objectives and understanding.

David Mooberry
Senior Vice President, The DuPont Company

If you want a consultant who is knowledgeable in virtually every aspect of business (sales, manufacturing, finance, marketing and administration), Bill is ideal. He is mature and calm under pressure. He has boundless energy and he is honest with everyone in every situation. My experience with Bill as a consultant was outstanding. Within a few weeks, Bill identified all of the problems, discussed alternatives with the owners and worked actively with us on the implementation. Bill had the ideas and the energy to make all of the changes which were necessary.

Stanley Snow
Owner, Snows, Inc.

In 1974, during the oil crisis, Bill came up with a recommendation to add Honda and BMW to our Pontiac franchise. Over the years these additions proved to be very profitable and allowed Union Park to generate millions of dollars in additional sales, service and parts business.
In 1979, Bill's leading edge marketing campaign on Pontiac for our dealership was the cause of our great increase in sales during the two years of the campaign. Receiving the EFFIE Award with Bill at the American Marketing Association meeting at the Waldorf Astoria in New York City was exciting since it is the most prestigious marketing award in the U.S.

Frank Ursomaro
President, Union Park, Inc.

Bill's enthusiasm, energy and intelligence mark him as a person with superb leadership qualities. People like to work with Bill and enjoy teaming with him because success is usually the result. Bill's breadth of experience sets him apart and enables those with more narrow experiences to leverage his. This adds to Bill's value as a business partner and an agent of change.

James Donaghy
Sheldahl, CEO

Bill is an innovative and clear thinker always looking for new ways to approach problems. His prime attributes are taking complex management problems, reducing them to a few key needs, and in helping to develop a clear, simple plan to execute.

Ned Jackson
Telex, CEO

Bill has an amazing ability to always remain creative even under the most pressing circumstances. He is a very good listener regardless of how rambling discussions might become. Through it all, Bill has the ability to see the big picture and also pay the necessary attention to detail. He constantly impressed us with his innovative ideas, his excellent interpersonal skills and his management knowledge. We worked together for ten years on marketing, personnel issues, strategic planning and all business matters that a quickly growing and then maturing business encounters.

Michael Uffner
President, Delaware Cadillac

In my opinion Bill is a bright, insightful consultant who has the ability to understand a given business problem and help the client work through to a solution. He is intelligent, analytical and persistent. He is always very well organized and responsive. He places high value on being able to keep his commitments and deliver on time. In addition to these virtues, Bill is a nice person to be with. He is unfailingly cheerful and upbeat, and his ready sense of humor is a welcome addition to the business setting.

Dennis Hykes
Principal, CFO Solutions, Inc.

I have found Bill to be a thoughtful, organized, and caring person with an infectious positive attitude. He has a wealth of knowledge which he has garnered from many varied business and educational experiences. Bill is an accomplished public speaker and an effective educator. He leads not only by sharing his knowledge with others, but also as an example of the standards by which he lives. Bill is a valued resource who brings a fresh point-of-view to a complicated business world.

Jerry Hoganson
Administrator, St. Paul's Church Home, Inc.

Bill is a wonderful role model as a strong, energetic leader. His creativity and optimism always come through and help motivate others during good and difficult times alike. In addition to being a big picture thinker, he demonstrates a wonderful ability to explore different options, when appropriate.

Yigal Ron
President, MultiMed

"Peace-of-Mind" Series by Bill Peter

Book One:

"Peace-of-Mind" (our home).

"I'M MOVING" - **Eliminating the anxiety of bu   ıg or selling a home.**

Book Two:

"Peace-of-Mind" (our work).

Unleashing Business Creativity...to empower your clients.

Book Three:

"Peace-of-Mind" (our moral behavior).

As the Soul Teaches.

Printed in the United States of America.

Library of Congress Catalog Card Number: 99-67932

ISBN 1-890676-49-7

Beaver's Pond Press, Inc.
Minneapolis, Minnesota

"UNLEASHING BUSINESS CREATIVITY

...to empower your clients."

Bill Peter

Beaver's Pond Press, Inc.
Minneapolis, MN

Preface

"Peace-of-Mind" at Work

The Chief Executive Officer (CEO) must also be the Chief Empowerment Officer (CEO) if a business is going to evolve to Unleashing Business Creativity.

Find an organization with a sincere Chief Empowerment Officer, a worthy mission, enthusiastic and empowered associates (which brings loyal and empowered clients) and you have found an organization where you can be creative, thoroughly enjoy your work and have "Peace-of-Mind."

Work occupies such a major portion of our life that we need to find a very emotionally satisfying career to be at peace. We all possess certain individual skills and talents and can improve them over time through education and experiences. Organizations have needs for skilled associates who will share in their vision. When a business and a group of associates share a common vision and are aligned emotionally so that the associates are comfortable dedicating their energies to the accomplishment of the company's mission, the associates and the business all benefit.

"Peace-of-Mind" is available to the CEO who recognizes the importance of being the Chief Empowerment Officer and leads the company by enlisting associates to share in the business mission and empower their clients. The Chief Empowerment Officer is responsible for empowering associates to empower clients. If clients do not feel empowered by one company, they can readily take their business elsewhere.

In government, officials must empower the citizens by providing them with pertinent information on key decisions and seeking their advice on what actions they want from their government. The voting power is available to the citizens to change their leaders. Creative leaders describe their vision to the citizens and involve the citizens in the refinement of the vision.

Whether you are in business, government, medicine, education or church, leaders need followers. Followers will be enthusiastic about their leaders when the leaders describe worthy visions, value the energies and ideas of their associates and involve them in the creation of the vision.

"Peace-of-Mind" occurs at work when our everyday activities are consistent with our personal value system. If we cannot be comfortable with a company's mission and values, we should strive to change them or dedicate our energies to another business.

Bureaucracy is one of the most serious barriers to the empowerment of associates and clients. Bureaucracy needs to be avoided like the plague in order to unleash the creative energies of all the associates. Minimizing bureaucracy also is very cost effective for an organization and serves clients by making the company responsive to the marketplace.

To live the creative life at work you uniquely were meant to live—that is "Peace-of-Mind."

Dedication

This book is dedicated to the many associates I have worked with over the years. They have taught me by their attitudes and behaviors that the true core competency of every organization is within its associates.

A special thank you to Aubrey Marion, who challenged me in 1958 with these words: "If I'm your technician and conduct the experiments that you design, and you are an 'A' performer in the company, how is it that I am a 'C' performer?" I mumbled and fumbled as a young engineer to answer Aubrey. Today I would say, "Aubrey, we did it together and both deserve the credit. We were partners, co-workers, I'll say 'associates' in the work. We needed each other's skills to end up with good results."

Thank you Aubrey, and all the other associates I have had the pleasure to work side-by-side with in the world of business in thousands of situations.

Thanks To My Supporters

Unleashing Business Creativity was exciting to assemble with the help of many people, as Book Two in the "Peace-of-Mind" Series.

My wife, Arlene, deserves special thanks for her great patience and support. Draft after draft of the text were made possible through the excellent help of Virginia Matzinger. Ryan Soderstrom and Daniel Verdick were outstanding in their efforts on the overall design of the book, its production and marketing.

Suggestions for improvement on early drafts were extremely valuable from Milt Adams, Peter Hovde, Dennis Hykes, Ned Jackson, Julie Olson, Lynn Schleeter and Paul Schmidt.

Thanks to all for the great encouragement and support.

Table of Contents

The Market Opportunity   Page

Creative Corporate Culture

Creative Strategies And Tactics

OVERVIEW

Creativity comes from within. We experience, we learn, we remember, we dream, and in wondrous new ways, we create new thoughts, new approaches and new concepts.

1

Unleashing Business Creativity: Summary

Unleashing business creativity is unleashing the power within your associates to empower your clients.

We know that every single human being is creative, once they permit themselves to be and once their business organizations realize the power available within every individual.

The role of managers is to define the mission and vision for a business with the input from many associates, and then to unleash the business creativity of all their associates by establishing an atmosphere that encourages, celebrates and rewards creativity.

The lessons of the business world are simple and straightforward:

1. Passion is needed to define a worthwhile mission and vision.

2. Dedication and persistence are essential to follow the vision.

3. Unleashing the creativity of all of your business associates to fulfill the mission and vision is critical to a business' profitable growth.

4. In all actions, the character and integrity of the leader is essential to empower associates to enthusiastically join the challenge by fully utilizing their creative talents to empower the clients.

Unleashing Business Creativity was born of forty years of varied business experiences. The stories and lessons on a wide range of business subjects all have a common theme— the power within your associates is the key to your business success and the key to your "Peace-of-Mind" at work.

This book has been written for everyone who works in the businesses of the United States in every job—not just executives.

Consider spring training for a baseball team. Everyone, the rookies and the stars, go through the ritual of returning to fundamentals. Why? Because experience has shown the baseball managers, owners and players that the players' skills get rusty over the winter. Everyone has something to learn and/or relearn; fundamentals are the solid foundation.

In a business, creativity is critical. Everyone throughout the organization develops the great innovations, if they are encouraged to do so by the owners or leaders of the organization. The early chapters of this book should be read as spring training…well-known to the experienced person in business, but important to always remember.

Chapter 2 and the chapters at the end of the book offer some concepts about which experienced managers will probably find more to think about and challenge. The ideas that are most important to you depend upon your previous experience in the business world. By the time you have completed the book, my wish is that you will have refreshed your memory on some important points and addressed some fresh new ideas.

Unleashing Business Creativity is a book written for everyone in a business, not just the executives. In fact, the best value of the book may be the feedback that the executives hear from the hundreds or thousands of their associates as the associates try to unleash their creativity and empower the clients. Everyone can be a winner in this process!

The stories and people in *Unleashing Business Creativity* are based on real business experiences and real people. In 60 percent of the chapters, new approaches are introduced in an intimate manner, as if the reader is overhearing business conversations. You know people and situations like those described in *Unleashing Business Creativity*. The names are different than the person or people who were involved in the original situations, but the learnings to be absorbed are as rich as I could make them. For every chapter, there are thousands of other examples; business life is full of creative people and creative solutions.

Creativity

Not just artists can be creative.
Musicians can. Doctors can. Lawyers can. Plumbers can.
Salespeople can. Teachers can. Business managers can.
Secretaries can.
Real estate agents can.
You can...and how!!

We saw a block of granite next to a beautiful granite eagle and asked the artist how he had created the eagle.
"I looked at the block of granite and chipped away the part that wasn't an eagle," he said.
That's vision and that's creativity.
Creativity comes from within. We experience, we learn, we remember, we dream, and in wondrous new ways...we create new thoughts, new approaches and new concepts.
Every mind is creative and imaginative, excited by new possibilities in all parts of life's experiences.
Our Creator gave us the inner ability to be creative in our world of material things and relationships.
How creative and imaginative we can be; it is like exciting music is pulsing through our veins.
How creative and enthusiastic we can be; it is an exhilaration for our body and soul.
A business is a group of people pursuing a common vision.
To do it creatively makes the pursuit more exciting and emotionally enriching.
Everyone can be creative in their work and enjoy a rich life in the process.
Creativity and "Peace-of-Mind" at work is a route to excitement and satisfaction.

It is kind of fun to do the impossible.
Walt Disney

The client is in the center of the Client Empowerment Mindset™; the client is not even visible in the Pyramid Paradigm.

2

The Client Empowerment Mindset™

The pyramid has been the primary organizational paradigm or model, but as we enter the new millennium, the Client Empowerment Mindset™ will be a more attractive alternative for many.

The pyramid symbolism has penetrated all phases of our society, our language and our behavior. We talk of people in charge as being at "the top" and workers being at "the bottom."

We have many hierarchies:

- General, captains, sergeants, privates
- Cardinals, bishops, priests, parishioners
- Vice presidents, directors, managers, employees

We talk of "climbing up the ladder" and "advancing to a higher level." And we admire people with a "big job" managing many people who have made it up through the "glass ceiling."

We have experienced bureaucracies that are sometimes stifling to the people trying to do an excellent job within

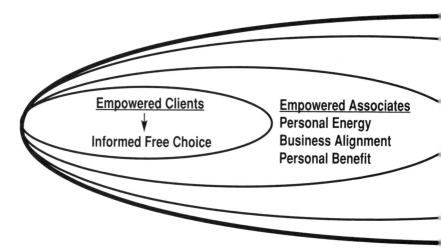

organizational policies that:

a) reward those who follow all the established rules, and

b) are not always friendly to creative innovation.

The Client Empowerment Mindset™ is a dramatically different model which, I submit, is more in tune with the challenges ahead for us as growing individuals in a growing society. As we reach the year 2000, it is time to reevaluate our organizational thinking and explore the Client Empowerment Mindset™.

MOST IMPORTANTLY, THE CLIENT IS IN THE CENTER OF THE CLIENT EMPOWERMENT MINDSET; THE CLIENT IS NOT EVEN VISIBLE IN THE PYRAMID PARADIGM.

The focus of attention for all organizations (businesses, governments, schools, etc.) within the Client Empowerment Mindset™ concept is on the empowered clients. Clients deserve to have the ultimate power exercised through their informed free choice (see graphic above).

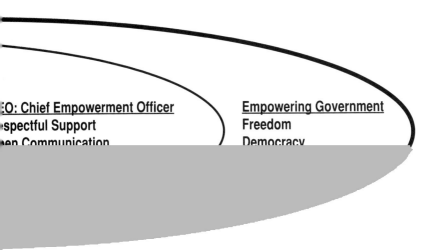

CEO: Chief Empowerment Officer
Respectful Support
Open Communication

Empowering Government
Freedom
Democracy

Empowered associates have the primary responsibility of empowering the clients. Empowered associates focus their personal energy in alignment with the goals of their business because they see a personal benefit in doing so—personal growth, career enjoyment and satisfaction in having empowered the clients.

The CEO (Chief Empowerment Officer) leads effectively when all of the associates throughout the organization are focused on empowering clients. The tools of the CEO are respectful support, open communication and avoiding bureaucracy.

Freedom, democracy and the free enterprise system are the essential components of the empowering government we enjoy in the U.S.A. This is consistent with the familiar phrases "of the people, by the people and for the people" and "consent of the governed."

Summary

The focus of the Client Empowerment Mindset™ is on the empowered clients.

God gave us memories so that humans could be connected with the past.
Mike Ruhland

"Associates" and "clients" are more than just words; they carry positive meanings that are helpful to the thinking of business managers, now and into the future.

3

Language and Meaning

Employees	→	Associates
Customers	→	Clients

Language changes over time. Sometimes words take on new meanings (for example, "grass" used to be found on a green lawn and now "grass" has another common slang meaning for marijuana).

Over the years, many "employees" have been called "associates." It is not just a modern term; "associates" has a broadly different meaning. An "associate" is an equal; it is used to refer to coworkers, part of a team effort, whereas an "employee" still has the connotation of being a secondary and sometimes adversarial role (as in "management and employees"). Disney calls their "associates" by the term "cast members" at their amusement parks. "Cast members" has a very important meaning; Disney emphasizes in their training programs that they are in the entertainment business.

For the past fifteen years, I have thought of the framework of "associates" as the preferred mental set. In writing this book, I have been debating which term to use to convey meaning most effectively. I have chosen to use "associate."

Over time, it is my hope that "employee" will become a less popular term as we strive to unleash the business creativity and the power from within our associates to empower our clients.

Similarly, I feel "client" is a much more powerful term than "customer." We all are familiar with the term "customer," which is commonly used in retail sales and industrial sales. "Client" is the term frequently used by lawyers, accountants, real estate agents and consultants. They receive compensation for their services from their "clients." Doctors and nurses refer to the people they care for as "patients," if they are in the clinic or in the hospital, and "residents," if they are in a long-term care facility (old language: nursing home).

Since this is a book primarily about business, I will use the term "client" throughout. I am hopeful that the "client" concept will become stronger as a result in the reader's mind. A "customer" has a connotation of possibly having a minimal relationship dimension with your business. However, a "client" has a stronger relationship dimension. My preference is for the word "client" because all businesses prefer to develop strong long-term business relationships with their "clients/customers."

"Associates" and "clients" are more than just words; they carry positive meanings that are helpful to the thinking of business managers, now and into the future.

I always have choices and sometimes it is only a choice of attitude.
Judith Knowlton

Take on new investments carefully as the business grows, watch the increase in expenses in good times and price high enough for a reasonable profit, gauging the value of your offering carefully.

4

Profit Is a Clean Word

A pushcart peddler on the streets of New York once said, "Business is really easy. You buy for cheap, sell for high and don't invest too much in the pushcart."

The peddler's statement is disarmingly simple. Every manager knows this simple principle, but how many times is this principle forgotten in the pressure of everyday decisions?

Let's start with the pushcart. Businesses require some form of investment to get started. The peddler might have suggested that you rent a used pushcart first, then when the business has grown, buy a used pushcart and eventually, when business is quite good, buy a new pushcart. The key is having a minimum adequate investment to do the job. However, so often in our businesses we want the best and we want it up front. Our egos are satisfied by having the best, but it isn't necessarily the correct business judgment to invest a great deal in a new business.

Greg Shell was a man with a very strong empire-building ego. To him large, impressive looking buildings were symbols of success and prestige. Greg encouraged his company to build facilities aggressively because, he argued, it was the only way to attract good people, and good people were going to be the basis of a successful business. One building Greg's coworkers dubbed the "Gregory W. Shell Memorial" because it was never filled with people. The business did not succeed to match Greg's dreams, and the building eventually had to be sold. Buildings are important. Plant equipment is important. But more important is the concept of earning as you grow. Large expenditures up front in a business need to be carefully scrutinized. Do you have some Gregs in your organization? Are you using minimum adequate investments to get the job done? Are you renting some facilities or equipment until you are confident the business will support the investment? What approaches do you have to justify major new investments Are they as rigorous as the pushcart peddler's criteria?

Now, on to buy for cheap, sell for high. Buy for cheap is a shorthand way to say watch your expenses carefully. Purchases of raw materials are certainly part of producing product, and most organizations pay a reasonable amount of attention to getting dependable and low-cost suppliers. But buy for cheap suggests that all expenses need to be watched carefully in good times and bad times. How many times have you known a business to hit some bad times and conclude, as Betty Baxter did: "We had a lot of fat. Our organization was over staffed during the upturn in the economy. We would have been wiser to have added people and facilities more slowly. Our fixed costs were so high that, when sales decreased somewhat, we quickly went into a loss position. The next time we will know better."

How many business ups and downs have you been

through? How many times have you said, "We added too much overhead and variable costs during the up period." It seems that we tell ourselves that the next time we will know better, and yet we do not resist the temptations of dramatic expense growth in up times. Why? No one likes a wet blanket! When things are going well, the management team is up and hiring. It is not at all popular to be a member of such a management team and be a wet blanket, saying growth in costs should be watched. We all tend to want to be optimistic about the future. But who will provide a sense of balance to a management team? Will you? Should you? Controlling expenses in down times is easy; you just go along with what everyone sees. Controlling expenses in up times takes good judgment, courage and leadership. Have you got the courage and leadership needed to control business expenses in up cycles?

Sell for high was the last piece of advice from the peddler. He was not saying to charge an unreasonably high price. We all know that if we price our product or service too high in proportion to its value to clients and in comparison to competitive offerings, our volume will decrease and our market share will decline. The peddler was saying, "Don't charge less than a well-informed client would consider a fair price."

What goes through your mind when you see a product that you have seen routinely selling for $100 available for $40? Something must be wrong with this item. It must have a physical defect, or if it looks satisfactory, something else must be wrong with it. The manufacturer must be dumping it for some reason. It must be an old model they could not sell. If they couldn't sell it to other people, why should I take a chance? An $80 price for an item which normally sells for $100 can be perceived as a good buy; a $40 price may well be perceived as a bad buy.

The peddler would suggest that business managers understand their product or service offering, what competitors offer, and what the clients value. Then, the peddler would suggest that the price be high enough to make a reasonable profit but low enough to be considered a fair price. Lasting business relationships and repeat purchases depend on fair pricing in comparison to the product or service value.

The wisdom of the peddler is so simple, but we so often forget to apply it. Take on new investments carefully as the business grows, watch the increase in expenses in good times and price high enough for a reasonable profit, gauging the value of your offering carefully.

At her retirement, a very successful multi-millionaire was asked to identify the key to her business success. She said, "When I was a young woman, a successful business person told me to always make a 20 percent margin…so I always did." "How did you calculate your margin," she was asked. "Oh, you know, anything I bought for a dollar, I sold for five dollars." Math Grade: F ; Business Acumen Grade: A.

Every business starts with a person with vision who starts small, takes a big risk, manages it well, employs associates for many years and offers useful products and services that are appreciated in the marketplace by the clients buying them.

Profit is important to sustain a business. With profit, a company continues to serve clients, employ associates and

return some money to the shareholders who took the risk to
fund the business.

Clients, associates and investors are the three key audi-
ences for a business. All three must be served in a balanced
manner to have a company that is healthy long term.

**Happiness does not depend on what we have, but on
who we are.**
Henry van Dyke

The simple solution is simple in hindsight; only a great deal of imagination leads to finding the simple solution.

5

Business from the Creative Trenches

Business is all about markets, products, services, leaders, competitors, prices, profits, people, egos, politics, judgments, morale and vision. The world of business is as exciting as a new product and as exhilarating as a new challenge successfully met by hard and creative work.

We sometimes strain to find the complex interactions of many variables only to eventually conclude that the simple solution is the most profound. Of course, the simple solution is simple in hindsight; only a great deal of imagination leads to finding the simple solution. And often there are several simple, practical solutions to business problems and opportunities.

Upon reflecting on years of working with business people, some simple and perhaps profound principles stand out as helpful. As a practitioner in the business world, you will recognize most of these principles.

There is a time for reflection, when we get to the core of things. Business is "serious" and it is "fun" to us who participate in this exciting world. It is more than production lines, computer programs, home office planning meetings, happy and unhappy clients. It is as exciting as the game of living and, after all, it should be—we spend most of our waking hours worrying about and enjoying our business activities. We seek "Peace-of-Mind" at work.

This book is not a textbook on managing a business, yet it is a valuable resource every member of an organization can read to get a good sense for the full managing experience. This book is a collection of many business principles, which are sometimes best explained in the form of everyday conversations that would be overheard in any company. My attempt is to communicate in plain English with real life experiences.

The deepest principle of human nature is the craving to be appreciated.
William James

Creative Business Vision & Leadership

When a manager has knowledge, vision, leadership and integrity, the sum of those strengths inspire associates to dedicate their collective energies to the business.

6

Managing Creatively

Managing creatively in a business is a task requiring knowledge, vision, leadership, integrity and passion. This book was written with the practicing business manager in mind. Others in all parts of organizations will find the book fascinating because of its vivid description of the everyday world of the manager in business. Managing is an intellectual challenge, a challenge to a person's interpersonal relations skills, and a challenge to a person's ethical and moral behavior. Trust among associates is the key to an effective team effort.

KNOWLEDGE:

The newcomer to the business world asks, "How did you know that the competitors would react in that way when we introduced our new program?" The seasoned manager has accumulated knowledge from education, years of experience, reading, talking with other business people, thinking through the potential decisions along with the risks and benefits, and so on. What a seasoned manager calls a hunch or a feeling is frequently an educated summary of knowledge of the business world and what makes it tick. Knowledge can be taught

31

and accumulated, but no lesson is so well remembered as a personal, firsthand experience. Experience is an outstanding teacher for the prepared mind that is constantly seeking to learn more business principles.

VISION:

Edwin Land from Polaroid had vision when he imagined instant photography. John F. Kennedy had vision when he challenged the country to the manned space program. The first company that started plastic charge cards had vision. Bill Gates had vision in software for personal computers. The founders of the Internet had vision. The developers of rapid mail delivery and electronic mail had vision. Vision in a business manager frequently takes less dramatic forms than the ones just described, but it is a necessity. It is critical for a manager to have a mental picture of where he or she wants the business to go before taking it there. A manager without vision is just an administrator. Effective administration is valuable; effective management toward a meaningful vision is a distinguishing characteristic of a good leader. A good leader also is flexible to alter the vision, if necessary, as new situations evolve over time.

LEADERSHIP:

Effective management is effective leadership, and leadership must be assessed from all sides, with the view of the followers being extremely important. So often we look to the organization structure, and somewhere at the top, we expect to find the leader. An organization is only at its peak effectiveness if leadership abounds throughout the organization—not in counterproductive and different directions, but in creative problem solving aligned toward a meaningful vision. Leadership is as difficult to measure as it is to describe. You know it when you see it, but it often takes different forms. A leader can be quiet or flamboyant, humble or proud, aloof or friendly. But a leader always has a presence that others respect and are willing to follow. Leadership is not a natural-born quality since we all come into the world alone; so it is a learned quality based on family and all other social and intellectual experiences. Leadership is about character and integrity.

INTEGRITY:

Integrity or character are critical dimensions of a leader who is an effective manager. If not at first, people can eventually detect lack of sincerity, honesty, integrity - character. If a manager cannot be trusted or trust others, there are serious questions about his or her effectiveness as a manager. In the absence of integrity in the leader, a follower is prudent not to take risks.

Unleashing Business Creativity contains business principles woven into examples of real people's business experiences in such a way as to highlight how KNOWLEDGE, VISION, LEADERSHIP and INTEGRITY can be utilized for a powerful combination…the excitement of managing and unleashing business creativity.

PASSION:

When a manager has knowledge, vision, leadership and integrity, the sum of those strengths usually exemplifies itself as passion—dedication, enthusiasm, persistence, confidence, positive attitude—qualities which inspire his or her associates to dedicate their collective energies to the business. With passion, the leader seeks to unleash business creativity to empower clients.

> **Our memory is powerful; you forget—it doesn't. It simply files things away. It keeps things for you or hides things from you...and summons to your recall with a will of its own. You think you have a memory, but it has you.**
>
> John Irving

A good businessperson is careful not to think that he or she has a strong position when many other offerings compete to fill the same need.

7

What Business Are We In?

Jim Nichols manufactures and sells steel-centered golf balls. What business is he in? Steel-centered golf balls? Golf balls? Golf equipment? Sporting equipment? Balls? Or what?

Some managers would argue that it is foolish to debate what business Jim is in; he clearly is in the golf ball business. Jim Nichols' company is the major supplier of steel-centered golf balls. He has 60 percent of the steel-centered golf ball market but only 2 percent of the total golf ball market and less than 0.5 percent of the golf equipment market.

Other managers would want to know more about Jim Nichols' business before they judged what business he is in. Does Jim also make golf bags, golf clubs, or golf carts? Does he sell any products that other manufacturers produce so he can complete his offering to his clients? Who does he consider his clients to be? Who does he consider his major competitors to be?

Many products of different design can fill the same need. For example, boards can be connected with nails, screws, bolts, glue, and so on. Clothing can be made of a variety of different fabrics. At death, cremations compete with coffins and burials. A good businessperson is careful not to think that he or she has a strong position when many other offerings compete to fill the same need.

In construction, wood competes with plastic, steel, glass, and concrete, and so on. One clue to what business you are in can be derived from studying the comments of your clients. If they sometimes switch from your product to another, then you compete with that product and your business definition has to comprehend the competitive product as well as yours.

Jim Nichols tells a fascinating story: "I knew one business that told its management for three years that it had 100 percent of a market. This business had a patented product that only they produced so, by definition, they sold 100 percent. They had 100 percent product share but gradually their market share went from 5 percent to 2 percent and later down to 1 percent. Any market, of which you have 100 percent, is definitely incorrectly defined. This patented product led management to think they had a strong business when it was very weak in the competitive marketplace.

By listing the products we sell, the products we compete with, the markets we sell into and the markets we do not penetrate, we can begin to clarify what business we are in. That sounds so simple, but it is the core of all strategic management. Of course, after defining where we now sell, the strategic question is, "Where do we choose to sell certain product or service offerings?"

Sometimes businesses hire consultants to help them wrestle with the future strategic direction of their business. It is important for a management team to decide if it wants to use a prescriptive consultant (to give them some recommendations based on his or her experience) or a facilitating consultant (who will challenge the management team to do most of their own creative thinking and planning).

Defining what business Jim Nichols is in is not as easy as it first seemed. It never is, but it is critical for the effective strategic planning of any company. Where are you in your business? If your key managers were asked what business they are in, would they all answer the same way? If they wouldn't, does that indicate to you that you have a problem to solve? Perhaps the Jim Nichols' example will help.

Jim Nichols generalized, "When businesses elect to expand their scope to new products and/or new markets, they are considering the following grid, with the company's established products and established markets being in the upper left hand corner and the growth described as 'market penetration.' The other boxes describe the nature of 'product development,' 'market development' and 'new business development.' "

CHANCES OF BUSINESS SUCCESS

	Established Products	New Products
Established Markets	Market Penetration	Product Development
New Markets	Market Development	New Business Development

"It is important to recognize," continued Jim, "that the chances of business success are highest where you understand the products and markets. The chances of business success reduce to only about 50 percent with new products, about 25 percent in new markets and 5 percent in brand- new business areas."

CHANCES OF BUSINESS SUCCESS

	Established Products	*New Products*
Established Markets	75 percent	50 percent
New Markets	25 percent	5 percent

"Discussion of what businesses we are in and what businesses we want to be in opens up many strategic questions. Core competency is one of those key strategic questions," said Jim.

Only in growth, reform and change, paradoxically enough, is true security to be had.

Anne Morrow Lindbergh

A core competency is distinctive technology, marketing, product or a service competitive advantage that is not readily copied by competitors.

8

Core Competency

A concert pianist has a core competency that is obvious to an audience as they listen to the music and see the expression of intensity and joy of the performer. The pianist may not be very skilled at cooking or golf, but the core competency of performing at a peak level on the piano is evident to all, including the pianist.

The pianist's core competency has been developed and perfected over time with formal training and very extensive practice. Then, more training and more practice. Only with dedication does any professional become a leader.

Let's consider the core competency of a business. How do we recognize it? Where does it come from? How can it be improved, or how can it be lost?

A number of publicly held corporations have a market valuation that greatly exceeds their book value. An accountant generally calls this "goodwill" because it is a value beyond what can be supported with a financial evaluation of assets. Yet this very real market valuation is the result of investors who are judging that the company will continue to perform well in the future. Disney, Microsoft, Coca-Cola,

Intel, McDonald's, Johnson & Johnson, 3M, General Electric—many companies enjoy a significant market premium over book value. And if you study the companies, they have a common theme, a core competency—a focus on one or several market niches in which they lead and innovate.

When companies divest themselves of one of their divisions, they have often decided to return to their primary technology, market, services and products (their area of core competency). Therefore, a core competency is distinctive technology, marketing, product or a service competitive advantage that is not readily copied by competitors.

Core competency comes from people—leaders with a vision, managers facilitating that vision and many associates accepting the vision and aligning their personal goals with those of the business leaders to empower the clients.

Some companies focus on services, others focus on products, some operate only in the U.S., others worldwide. Over time, the products and services change as technology, laws and competitive offerings evolve.

But the common element in a core competency is the specific competency of the associates. Microsoft has a unique environment that attracts people who love to develop and market software. Coca-Cola has a unique environment that attracts people who love the soft drink business. If 10,000 experienced associates of Microsoft and Coca-Cola were swapped to the other company, both companies would suffer.

New products and services are developed by people who have a passion for their business, who have the skill to innovate and who have the emotional and financial backing of leaders who share the dedication to the market.

An interesting business story comes from Xerox. They had about sixty leading researchers at their Palo Alto Research Laboratory in 1973. They conceived of many of the prototypes for the personal computer industry and network systems that we know today. But Xerox didn't feel that such technology was part of their core competency in copy machines. Microsoft, Intel, Apple, IBM and others capitalized on the basic principles from Palo Alto, and twenty-five years later they (and not Xerox) have the core competencies as part of their companies. The core competencies, the knowledge and the skill is embodied in the associates.

Everything depends on the corporate culture and how it focuses attention on the clear definition of the core competency that it has now and what it is aiming for in its vision for the future. Leadership and all associates define and refine the corporate culture and, in the process, define the core competency needed for the future.

The Internet is an example of this concept. It is an exciting frontier, and companies compete to hire Internet experts. Salary is important in attracting staff, but the corporate culture and core competency already in existence in a company is also very important to a new hire and a long-time associate.

If I'm excited about the commodity grain business, I probably won't be attracted to General Motors. If I want to write a successful Broadway play, I'll find a way to learn from experts in that field. Similar minds get together and form a core competency for their company.

To develop a core competency and nurture it, the Chief

Empowerment Officer (CEO) needs to send clear signals to his or her organization on a consistent basis, and positive recognition needs to be evident for those who enhance the company's core competence.

Imagining the future to give your company a competitive advantage is the key step to enhancing the core competency of your associates.

Anyone who keeps the ability to see beauty is never old.
Franz Kafka

One product and one market is probably too narrow a focus for a company interested in long-term business health.

9

All The Eggs in One Basket

Leadership in a market has its rewards. Companies that offer unique products and services, enter a market early, and serve it in depth achieve excellent market positions and excellent earnings. However, one-product companies or one-market businesses run the risk of being so narrowly focused that they cannot stand the test of time and competition.

A great deal has been said about finding a market niche. Nick Nietske was eloquent in his description of his product and its market niche, "Nobody could touch us in the market. We started to provide our product two years before anyone else did. Our product became the standard for this market. All other products that were introduced later had to compare themselves to ours. We had 50 salespeople and 50 service representatives covering the whole country before our competitors had their first dozen people. What a great head start, and we enjoyed excellent earnings. Then we had two problems hit us at once. The total market shrunk during a recessionary period and our new competitors took a good share of what was left with very low prices. Our bottom line looked sick, and we had to lay off quite a few people. Sure, we expected that, over time, we could make a comeback with new offerings and a stronger overall economy. But we didn't have another product or another market to balance off our poor performance."

What had Nick done wrong? After all, he had followed the good advice to focus on a market niche to succeed. One product and one market is probably too narrow a focus for a company interested in long-term business health. Consider the following matrix:

		Markets					
		1	2	3	4	5	6
	A	I	I	I			
	B	II					
	C		II		III	III	III
Product	D		II	III			
/Service	E		II		III		
	F	IV		IV	IV	IV	IV
	G	II				IV	IV

Company I has product A in three markets. That certainly gives it more balance than if it had product A in only one market. The other three companies shown have diversified in other ways—several products to serve a market in depth or several products in several markets. All of these cases provide a more balanced portfolio than Nick Nietske's one-product, one-market company.

Notice, the four companies charted serve from three

(Company I) to seven niches (Company IV). If one company tried to serve all forty-two niches, they would probably spread themselves too thin and not be able to become the leader in most niches. Being the leader in one-product/one-market niche can be a good place to start, but it is not a stable position long term. Focusing is important, but too narrow a focus can lead to vulnerability.

Nick Nietske was a quick learner. When he joined his second company he decided to diversify somewhat. He talked to his next door neighbor who was in the insurance business. Nick asked, "Do you sell just auto insurance or do you also sell home insurance and life insurance? Once you have a client with one insurance, do you sell him another type?" "No," said the neighbor. "I'm an auto insurance specialist. My company feels that it is better for us to focus on just one product. It bothers me though. I spend a lot of time getting to know a client, and once I do, I wish I could sell him another insurance product. What I have to do is refer him to another one of the company's specialists if he wants some home insurance or life insurance. It is not like the insurance business is that complicated. I could handle all three, but that is not how we are organized."

Nick could hardly resist. He told his neighbor about his "all the eggs in one basket" experience and how he was changing his business approach with his new company. His experience, in general terms, was identical with his neighbor's in the insurance business. Nick asked his neighbor, "What about your competitors—do they only have their salespeople focus on one type of insurance?" "No," said his neighbor.

"And I feel it puts them at a competitive advantage. But I can't convince my management to change. Maybe I should have you join my boss and me when we have lunch next week." "I'd be delighted," said Nick. "The discussion on multiple niches should be as much fun as the lunch."

Do you have any Nick Nietske's in your company? Are you convinced that several selected niches is the best approach? How many niches can you be a leader in? Perhaps three to seven would be good for a starting goal. One niche may not be ideal, except at the very beginning. Forty-two may not be ideal either, unless you have a very large company and you are picking the forty-two from hundreds of potential niches.

I am only one, but I am one. I cannot do everything, but I can do something.
Helen Keller

Some managers and some companies are content to concentrate on the short term. Others are so focused on the long term that they miss some current earning opportunities.

10

A Bird in the Hand

A bird in the hand is worth two in the bush. Or am I being measured on near-term or long-term performance? Most associates concentrate their efforts on what management pays attention to.

"Everyone in my organization knows what our business goals are," stated Ruth Abrams. "We are all dedicated to increasing the company's earnings per share by 20 percent this year. Our main approach to reaching that goal is to sell 20 percent more product and maintain our present margin on each sale." Bob, a friend, asked Ruth, "How about next year and the next? Do you feel you can increase sales 20 percent per year over a ten-year period with today's product line, or will you need some new products?" Ruth stated with great firmness, "Look, Bob. They don't pay me to worry about ten years from now. My management has set the goal of 20 percent for this year, and they check my progress toward meeting my sales and margin goals every two weeks. At the end of the year, they won't ask me how well I did building for the future. They have told me this is the only year that counts for my next raise and bonus. New products just cost a lot of money, which would pull down my product line's earnings for this year. I will postpone thinking about new products to next year, when management feels the need to set that as a goal. If they do it, I sure hope they expect only a 10 percent increase in earnings that year. We cannot do everything at once."

Ruth's management has shown its goals by what they pay attention to. They might want Ruth to take a long-term perspective on the health of the business, but they are only inspecting the short-term indicators. People do what management inspects. What management *expects* is only made clear to their associates by what they *inspect*. Ruth is clear in her mind and she has conveyed it to her whole organization that short-term, one-year performance is what the entire organization should focus on. After all, that is going to be the criteria for their salary and bonus considerations.

The emphasis on short-term performance could be called the "bird in the hand is worth two in the bush" business philosophy. It has many supporters. In fact, many of the financial calculation methods used in business—discounted cash flow, net present value of a stream of year-by-year incomes and expenses and investors method return—make earnings in the early years more important than future years. The logic is very compelling. By having high earnings in the early years, the money made can be earning interest or reinvested in other money-making ways in future years. A dollar earned now is worth a lot more than a dollar earned five years from now. The interest a dollar earned now can make over the next five years makes it more valuable than a dollar made five years from now. Also, a dollar earned five years from now might not have the same purchasing power because of inflation in the five years. A dollar earned today might buy a dozen eggs whereas, after inflation, a dollar earned five years from now may only buy 6 or 8 eggs. So there are some sound business reasons for emphasizing the bird in the hand.

Do you have some Ruth Abrams in your business? They are dedicated associates who are doing their best to meet what they perceive to be management's goals. Their perception is only as good as the clarity with which management expresses its goals and the areas where management routinely reviews progress.

Is it possible to emphasize the future so much that no short-term earnings are generated? Of course! We have all experienced cases where management focuses on making the best product for the market and the engineers say they need just a few more experiments (which take time and money). A year goes by, then another year, and there are expenses but little or no income. A building is purchased, equipment installed and people hired. Still many expenses and no income. After three years, when the product is starting to be sold, large up-front expenditures have been made. A large risk has been taken. If the product is right for the market and competitors have not met the need a year before us, we could be in store for a good business. However, if over time, people and money expenditures have not been too productive, we could have a big problem to explain to our board of directors.

It is less risky to go for the short-term earnings if the task is defined by top management as meeting this year's criteria.

For a one-year period, special efforts can be mounted to raise sales and reduce expenses. There are many good reasons to capitalize on the bird in the hand. After all, there may not be two in the bush.

A real estate company president is asked to sell his friend's $200,000 house for a flat fee of $10,000 instead of the more usual 7 percent fee of $14,000. Assuming the friend insists on it, the real estate company president has to decide whether the short-term gain of $10,000 is worth the potential problems he will have with other clients who paid 7 percent last month or future clients who might ask for a special rate. The $10,000 sounds good for the short term. The problems with recent clients and potential future clients sound bad. He makes the judgment on the short- or long-term criteria he feels are most important. Although he likely will not make any extensive calculations, he will mentally build a cash flow model in his brain, calculate the net present value of the likely cash flow pattern over the years, and then make a decision. This whole process may only take 30 seconds. After all, he has to respond to his friend's request.

Some managers and some companies are content to concentrate on the short term. Others are so focused on the long term that they miss some current earning opportunities. Have you got the balance you want in your business? Whatever balance point you establish, be sure to communicate it clearly to your associates. Also, inspect the key areas that are important for you to establish the balance point where you want it throughout your organization. It is critical to have a common understanding of goals and yardsticks.

I realize that humor isn't for everyone. It's only for people who want to have fun, enjoy life, and feel alive.

Anne Wilson Schaef

.

Buy decisions are not without their problems. Every time you buy rather than make, the buy option still needs to be well managed.

11

Make Versus Buy

Every business needs some areas of expertise where it can have a competitive advantage (their area of core competence). Doing everything is often not as successful as making what you are best at and buying what others are best at. The egos of our associates generally urge us to "make." Often "buy" is the better business choice.

Forward and backward integration steps are examples of companies deciding to make rather than buy. Jerry Manning had an interesting approach in his business: "We had six people involved in managing our business who sat down monthly for three years to gradually refine our make-versus-buy decisions. Sometimes our decision to make was based on security. We felt that the key technology we were bringing to an offering was necessary to be done internally. Security is often a good criteria for make." Tom interrupted, "I agree with you on security, but it can be carried to extremes. My organization felt that janitor duty had to be done by associates rather than an outside janitorial contractor, and they stated the reason as security. Fortunately, we were able to convince them that we could lock up well and let the janitors do the cleaning less expensively than if we had to do it ourselves. Buy was better than make for us on janitorial services."

Jerry Manning continued with his explanation: "Of course, many of the parts of the product were not unique. We found that several outside vendors could produce those parts better and at lower cost than we could ourselves. The vendors had made large investments in special equipment, which were not justified for our scale. Buy was better than make." Tom questioned Jerry, "Didn't you see some advantages of producing all the parts in your own shop?" "Sure," said Jerry, "but we saved a lot of money by not having to expand our building, buy new equipment and hire skilled associates. Our business risk was lower this way. We could proceed with the product promptly and delay making a decision until it was a well-established business."

Jerry changed to another area—acquisitions. "When we considered buying two other companies we were making buy versus make decisions. We probably could have done the research ourselves, developed the products and services, developed the organization, convinced the clients to buy from us, and so on. The other approach was to acquire a company that had already gone through that cycle and was selling the product commercially. Time was important. They had clients and a market position now. We would have to develop one gradually. So we decided to buy one of the two companies after thorough analysis. The trouble was, they did not want to be part of a company such as ours, so they set a price so high, we elected to back away. We had decided to buy rather than make, but at the price they were asking, we decided to make."

Tom O'Brien chimed in, "At one point in our business, we had more financial people than sales people. It was amazing, we looked at the financial numbers thirty-six different ways, but our sales were dropping. Another buy versus make decision. We hired several distributors to supplement the sales force. That was buy rather than make for sales. And then, we reduced our financial staff by 50 percent, letting the analysis be done by existing home office people. We dropped a make in finance and it did not even cost us a buy."

"Staff jobs are good to look at for potential to buy rather than make," Jerry pointed out. "We found that on difficult legal questions our lawyers were required by the corporation to use outside counsel. A natural question is, why? Prestige of the outside counsel, better lawyers or what? When big decisions are involved that could go to court, the company liked to use outside counsel. It was a buy decision for comfort and psychological reasons."

Tom summarized, "So make versus buy can affect a lot of areas, purchase of materials, acquisition of companies, personnel staffing outsourcing."

"Yes," Jerry said, "and I want you to know that buy decisions are not without their problems. Every time you buy rather than make, the buy option still needs to be well managed. You can imagine what some suppliers can charge for only satisfactory services if you do not have someone managing the interface with them. Every buy decision requires continuing follow-up."

"I remember two beautiful cases of make decisions where the companies decided to make just enough of one of their raw materials to understand the technology and the costs involved. Then they negotiated with their regular suppliers from strength... 'We can make it ourselves for $1.30 per unit, but it is a headache. We'll be happy to buy from you for $1.50, but not the $2.00 per unit you offered.' Both cases helped the companies negotiate much better contracts with their suppliers. I guess you could call that make enough to creatively buy."

"We have an engineering group that wants to design something unique for us when a commercially available product is close enough to meet our needs. Should we make or buy?" "Jerry, you are asking me that," said Tom, "after all you have said about make versus buy?" "Well," said Jerry, "it isn't as cut and dried as it might sound. You are right in thinking we should buy since the available product meets our needs. But our engineers feel they can design something that will cost a lot less. That is what causes it to be tempting. We will be using thousands of those products over the years, and if we could save money on each one, it would be important to earnings." "Wait a minute," said Tom. "Have you considered what other useful work your engineers could be doing. Perhaps they could be used on your new product effort. Wouldn't the payoff be better to use their unique skills on new products? Also, don't you think, over time, you could get the product from a vendor and, through competitive forces, the cost per unit could be brought down?" Jerry responded, "Your points are well taken, Tom. I guess I got caught in the ego problem. You see, I worked quite a good portion of my career in engineering. I was proud of what unique designs we could develop. Looking at the make versus buy decision is harder when you have personal prejudices. Now that you highlight the real issues, I see where buy probably would have been better. But no, even with all my engineering bias, it will be better to buy."

Tom and Jerry—were they really on the right track on their make versus buy discussion? If you have decided to raise the make versus buy discussion more often, you probably have gotten the key value of Tom and Jerry's discussion. Every business needs a Jerry Manning to raise the issues. Are you a Jerry or do you have one on your staff?

Oh, the miraculous energy that flows between two people who take the risks of being totally open, of listening, of responding with the whole heart.
Alex Noble

THE MARKET OPPORTUNITY

We must keep our perspective that the ultimate objective is serving the clients. Without clients, there is no business.

12

The Client Is Boss

The client is truly your boss. Without his or her goodwill, there are no paychecks. Another way to look at this is that the client provides us our opportunity to serve —to use our skills and competencies to help others satisfy their needs.

Organizational hierarchies are built with first line contributors, supervisors, managers, general managers, vice presidents, and so on. In the day-to-day business world, we are sure that our job is to satisfy our boss. The boss is the boss because he or she is expected to lead a group to the satisfactory completion of objectives. The ultimate objective is to serve clients' needs at a reasonable profit. Therefore, the client is—in an overview look at business—the ultimate boss.

Bob Josephson was a bus driver who had his job carefully described to him—meet this exact schedule (be at the corner of Oak and Arch by 7:15 a.m. and at the next stop of Walnut and Arch by 7:19 a.m., and so on). He drove his route, had some problems with traffic and red lights and at the end of the day talked to his supervisor. Bob said, "The job is fine, the schedule can be met with a lot of concentration. But the worst part is the problem with the clients. Sometimes I have so many people waiting at a stop, and they don't have their fare ready. It makes me miss a light and be late for the next stop. I could make the schedule if it wasn't for the clients. In fact, I hit the schedule perfectly the last half of the route by skipping every other stop. The stops I passed had people waving angrily at me but, you understand, I just couldn't stop *and* keep on schedule."

This simple example probably has you saying, "Of course the client must be served; the client is paying the bus driver's pay." But how many times have you condoned poor client service in your business? No, not me! Yes, even you! How many clients are put on hold for longer than you would like when they phone into your business? How many have to wait longer than you would think reasonable for a delivery of your product? How many clients of yours have had their fill of some of your business policies? After all, you have a bus schedule to meet.

The client is always right. That statement conjures up a lot of emotion when business people discuss it. Many business people say, "You don't understand my clients. They gripe at anything. They're unreasonable. My business and my clients are very unique. If you feel we should have an attitude of the client always being right, you don't understand my business."

They are saying the same thing as the bus driver. Aren't they? "I could meet the schedule if it wasn't for the unreasonable clients."

Sure, things do not always go as we plan them in business. But we must keep our perspective that the ultimate objective is serving the clients. Without clients, there is no business and therefore no paychecks.

Imagine the real estate salesperson who is not available to show a house on Sunday when an out-of-town couple can be in town to look at the house. The client's schedule is fixed. The real estate salesperson needs to make some adjustments to accommodate the client's schedule needs. And if she does not, she will lose the sale.

But what about jobs in business that do not directly interface with clients? Do you ever wonder who in the back office of the bank or the telephone company designed your bill format that is hard to understand? Or how about the research engineer who designs a product to meet his criteria but misses the ease-of-repair criteria that are important to you? Or the dishwasher in a restaurant who does not inspect carefully enough and you end up with dirty silverware? They work in supporting roles and need to do their jobs in such a first-class, quality manner that they would be proud to face the client directly with the service they have provided.

The client is the ultimate boss, and this attitude in the minds of all our associates can be an extremely valuable one. We need to train our Bob Josephsons to be client oriented bus drivers. You know some good Bob Josephsons who might adjust their schedule on a day with heavy snow and rain, but they do not pass by clients waving.

Think about it. Where do you stand in your business? Where do you want to be? What level of client service is going to keep your business profitable for a long time?

Destiny is not a matter of chance;
it is a matter of choice.
William Jennings Byan

Segmenting a market into several groups having relatively similar buying behavior patterns is critical to the success of a business. Share of mind comes before share of market.

13

Positioning and Segmenting

Owning an important niche in the minds of a segment of clients is an extremely valuable business asset. Wouldn't it be helpful to know what niche your company's product or service owns in the minds of your clients and prospects?

When we make a buying decision, do we really do it rationally? Do we take the time and effort to find out what products are available in the whole world, what their key benefits are related to our needs and what their prices are related to our budget? It would be difficult to purchase a candy bar if we had to make a worldwide survey first! Of course, what we really do when we want to buy an insurance policy, some toothpaste, a hamburger, a new car, a refrigerator, a corporation's stock, a haircut, or any product or service—is first refer to our data bank and the impressions in our mind. If I had never heard about a tractor that could go 70 miles per hour and plow a large field in 30 minutes, that information is not in my brain so I make my tractor decision based on the information I have in my mind. The 70-mile per hour tractor might be a great buy for my needs, but if I have never heard about it from an ad, a friend or a salesperson, I cannot consider it in the decision-making process.

So each of us searches our brain when we are in the market for a product. If my brain says the best four cars for my needs are A, B, C or D, I am likely to see what the local car dealers for these four makes have available on the market now. I am not likely to travel 100 miles to buy a car because I strongly suspect it will need some service and, at least during the warranty period, I want as few headaches as possible getting it to a service center. So if only three of the four makes have a dealership reasonably close to me, the fourth has been eliminated from my search for a car because of distance.

Our minds are bombarded with stimuli of communications trying to sell us products and services. We see newspaper ads, magazine ads, direct mail, TV ads and billboards. We hear about various products and services from friends, from salespeople, on the radio, and by telephone. We see signs for various businesses as we drive to work. We notice a bakery on the corner of Arch and Walnut, and that fact is stored in our brain. One day, when we are looking for a birthday cake, we recall that a friend of ours mentioned that they bought a great cake on Walnut Street. We put that together with our memory of seeing the bakery, and we stop by that store because it is only two blocks from our route to work. If the cake is of good quality and reasonably priced, our brain records it for future reference when we want some special baked goods. In fact, while in the store we saw they were busy and many people were buying their fresh baked bread and rolls. And so it goes—we get impressions in our brain from many sources.

Once we have found a good bakery, we program that in our brain and we tend to turn it into a habit; we almost always go to that bakery. There are so many decisions to make that we find it very comfortable to turn many product or service decisions into routines so we can focus on new issues. If we are wrestling whether or not to buy a personal computer, what brand to buy and what store to buy it in, that takes some effort. Meanwhile, our routine purchases continue more or less as a habit.

Industrial products are no different. If a processing plant buys 1,300 different products and services, from fuel oil and machine parts to janitor services, some will become routines and some will be under active study with several different vendors contending for the business. As a supplier, it is critical to know when your product or service has moved from the "purchase routine" list to the "up for grabs" list. How many times have you wished you had a chance to talk to a client about continuing to use your line when it was too late because the buyer had put your portion of the business up for grabs and your sales representative did not find out about it soon enough to avoid losing some business?

What we have been talking about is positioning. We need to keep a constant reminder in our clients' minds that we have one of the best products or services to meet their needs. We also need to remind our clients that our service, delivery, price, and so on, are filling their needs. If we do not remind them constantly, our competitors will take some or all of the business.

Positioning is related to communications. A key question

is what message about our offering do we want the client to have in his mind? And in many cases, there are five to ten members of the client's business who have some involvement in the final decisions. Some messages are incompatible and, therefore, are rejected by buyers. How many advertisements of products can you think of that talk about having the highest quality and the lowest price? Many messages like that reach a buyer and are rejected because, after years of buying experience on thousands of products, most buyers feel you generally get what you pay for. We do not expect a Mercedes to be as low priced as a Ford, but we do expect it to have a distinctive grille and excellent engineering. When we get it serviced, we expect it to cost more—even for just an oil change—than for a Ford.

Positioning is a critical business decision. How do we want our clients to view our offering? How do they view our offering now? How do we stand in the minds of the potential clients? If they have a ranking in their mind of various products, where does our offering stand? What share of mind do we have which will lead to a good share of market? How do we develop a good share of mind?

Before we go too far, we need to discuss segmenting as well as positioning. If we have 1,000 potential clients, we could theoretically say we have 1,000 minds to influence (or 10,000 minds where ten people are involved per decision). Actually, perhaps 20 percent have similar (not identical) needs that we could appeal to with one positioning message. They could all be in France, or all be large volume clients, or all be government agencies, or all use the service in a unique way in their plant—segments that we will want to speak to with a common positioning message through several media. In this simple case, we might have five segments with five positioning messages. Our competitors may be different in each segment. Our product or service offering may be different. We may sell through distributors to one segment, by mail to another and with a direct sales force to another.

Segmenting a market into several groups having relatively similar buying behavior patterns is critical to the success of a business. Positioning the offering clearly to each segment through all communication approaches is critical. We cannot promise everyone everything or it will not be believable. We need to focus our messages and, extremely importantly, we need to be consistent.

After many repetitions, we position a given product or service in our mind. The manufacturer or supplier needs to keep their message foremost in our minds. If the message changes, we have the opportunity to rethink our priorities. It might cause us to buy more because we like the new position better or buy less because it is no longer as attractive an offering as it was before. A supplier must be careful when sending out some new positioning messages. Sometimes it is best to leave one product with its present position and offer a completely different product to serve another position. That is why some toothpaste brands promise to prevent tooth decay, others promise to freshen your breath and others to make your smile bright by making your teeth whiter.

Marketing research work is critical in determining what is in your client or prospect's mind. Many marketing research techniques have been developed for finding out what people think about a variety of products or services by using questions of many different types. It is critical to know what the clients are thinking now and what you want them to think.

To be most effective in business, we need to define various segments, develop a positioning message for each segment (and the product or service to go with it), send the message, and then measure the new position our clients have in their minds for our offering. Share of mind comes before share of market.

Creative thinking may mean simply the realization that there is no particular virtue in doing things the way they have always been done.
Rudolf Flesch

When competitors are bidding for more volume with lower price or more service, the clients benefit.

14

The Hungry Competitor

Every business has some fixed and some variable costs. When sales dip, the fixed costs do not change immediately and earnings slip. The hungry competitor decides to take actions to improve sales.

And what is the most common action? It is to reduce some prices. After all, it is reasonable. We need more sales volume to keep our plant running or our office busy so our fixed costs can be spread over a larger sales base. In the short term, we cannot change our fixed cost structure, but we can change prices fairly quickly in the quest of some more volume.

In other terms, the hungry competitor is operating at a lower ratio of sales to capacity than he would like. How can a low sales to capacity ratio come about?

Sales can be low due to a loss in market share, which can be a sign of overall weakness of the product offering or marketing. Sales also can be low due to a weakness in the total market in a weak economy even though we are maintaining our market share. It is critical to gather data to determine which is the real sales problem. That is the numerator of the sales to capacity ratio. Capacity goes up when you open a new service department, expand a plant, and so on.

Without any change in sales, an increase in a company's capacity will trigger it to take some action to fill the capacity or almost fill it. Bill Campbell had a sign on his desk that said, "Volume Cures All Ills!" He believed it. He understood the principle of sales to capacity ratio and had found that a low ratio meant a lot of management questions. So when capacity went up or sales went down, either caused the ratio to go down and Bill jumped into action. Generally, the response was the common one—reduce the price to get more volume.

So the hungry competitor finds himself in a low sales to capacity ratio situation and decides to increase volume by cutting price. Other competitors won't sit tight and have their business taken away by a hungry competitor. Heavens no! Will they always react with a price cut? Not always, but frequently. Who wins? The clients. When competitors are bidding for more volume with lower price or more service, the clients benefit from the forces of supply and demand. The situation is dynamic; one company might gain some market share and another company lose it. The company that loses market share sees their sales to capacity ratio dropping and fights back, usually with lower prices. Of course, if one company finds they cannot seem to win back the sales, they sometimes reduce their capacity—close a service department, drop a product line, close a plant, sell off a portion of their business to someone else, and so on. The hungry competitor either has to increase sales or decrease capacity.

Throughout business, various sales to capacity ratios are discussed. In industrial production businesses, a plant is considered operating very full when it is operating at 85 to 90 percent of capacity. After all, some time is needed for equipment maintenance downtime and product line switches. However, a plant operating at 60 percent of capacity is a big problem with a lot of fixed costs and not enough unit production. Management begins to get concerned at 80 percent sales to capacity ratios, 70 percent is a problem, 60 percent a very serious problem and 50 percent is panic time.

Other than price reductions, what actions can be taken to increase the sales to capacity ratio? Advertising, promotions, or new products can stimulate sales. Generally it is to the advantage of the market leader to fight back a competitive price move with a non-price counter. If the leader has to reduce price to match a hungry, smaller competitor, the price reduction can affect many clients, some of whom were not directly threatened.

An advertising counter, as an example, may be a cost effective one for an industry leader. The cost of advertising per unit volume is likely much lower for the industry leader. However, advertising, promotions and new products may not work and even an industry leader has to decide if it is going to fight price reduction with price reduction. Here is where it is very important to know if the total market demand is down or just your company's sales. It is critical to know if your business is maintaining market share.

Another possible reaction to the hungry competitor is to reduce capacity—lay off some associates, close an office, and so on. Of course, this step should not be taken without a lot of care. A key question that management asks is, "How long will we expect to have this dip in sales? Is it a short-term or long-term problem?" The answer dictates the type of action to be taken.

A hungry competitor can be a new one who never participated in our market before. They have a lot of capacity and no sales. They are looking to get some business. They may be using a new product to enter our market. They may be offering some new services or lower prices. When a market is perceived to be profitable and growing at a good rate, it attracts many new competitors all looking for their share.

It is not uncommon for the various competitors to be projecting their share for the future and, if all were added, they would exceed the market opportunity by 50 to 100 percent. All cannot succeed and some finally will have to adjust their plans to obtain reasonable sales to capacity ratios. When the growth of a total market slows for whatever reason (technology, the economy, government regulations, and so on), some companies drop out, effectively reducing the available capacity and others can operate in somewhat more desirable circumstances for awhile.

The hungry competitor is a business reality that is with us in many circumstances. The actions we take depend upon our business position, the strength of our total offering with our clients and the expected duration of the sales softness.

Sometimes we are the hungry competitor. We need to keep in mind what the likely reactions will be as we make our move. Suppose, for example, we use the popular price entrance approach. What we could creatively do is get two-year contracts from each of the clients we sign up. With that approach possible in some markets but not in others, the competitive backlash is minimized—at least at the client level where we have signed two-year contracts. Guess what we find when we offer our two-year contract to some other clients? The entrenched suppliers have gotten there first. They may have lost some business in Kansas City, but they protected it in Chicago.

The hungry competitor could be you. If it is you or someone else, consider what is occurring with sales to capacity ratios and market shares before you take quick actions. Consider the non-price response when you are a market leader. Build up your capacity to meet the growth of the market—excessive capacity can be a problem when many competitors are attracted to a market. Also, watch the fixed cost structure. When sales dip, very high fixed costs lead to serious earnings problems.

The hungry competitor is a very fascinating and common business phenomenon.

To do good things in the world, first you must know who you are and what gives meaning to your life.
Paula Brownlee

Your clients need to be nurtured with new products, new services and new prices all the time. If you don't, a competitor will.

15

Preparing for the Future

The business that has very few new offerings can only survive if its competitors follow the same pattern and its clients have no other alternatives. Those situations are rare, so new products and services are critical to long-term business health.

How many times in your business have you heard this question, in one form or another, from a client: "What have you done for me lately?" "Sure," says our client, "you convinced me to buy your product four years ago, and I have continued to buy it each year. But now your competitors are offering some very good products, services and—oh, yes—better prices than you offer." "But we have given you a great deal of special assistance over the four years. We've bent over backwards to meet your needs. You will agree to that, won't you?" "Yes," responds the client, "but that's the past. Now my boss is asking me what we are going to do for the future. Your product, service and price are just not as good on balance as at least two of your competitors."

Now it is serious negotiation time and it may be too late with this client. But, in general, you may have fallen behind so much in your offering that it will not be easy to catch up. You had the leadership position, but you lost it with this client, and perhaps with many others.

"What have you done for me lately?" No matter how it is expressed by a client, it is a key question. Your clients need to be nurtured with new products, new services and new prices all the time. If you don't, a competitor will. The secret is preparing for the future and not being caught with an offering that is too small or too late. As an example, close collaboration with clients at their facilities is important in involving clients in product development.

Some businesspeople feel their most valuable asset is their clients. It is not an asset that normally shows up in a financial report, but it is critical. Clients served well buy more of what you have to sell.

So how can you be sure to be first to your clients with the new offering? You cannot always be first, but you want to be first most of the time, and a close second when you are not first. Third is not satisfactory. To be first you will have to prepare extremely well for the future.

A useful discipline is to assign one of your most creative people a one-week assignment on developing a plan to have a competitor dislodge you from your present position. What weaknesses would the competitor focus on? What product offerings would be best to capture your business? What government regulations could be better met with a different competitive offering? What prices would give you a big problem? Now, with that one week analysis, have your creative "competitor for a week" shock your management team with his or her recommendations. If that does not get your organization to become more responsive to the client and the market, assign another person to be another competitor for a week, or to be your largest client. By mentally changing roles, we can look at ourselves more critically and objectively.

Preparing for the future means constantly challenging ourselves. Three months without a serious questioning of objectives should be a maximum. Some new offerings take years to develop, and those need special attention.

We need to have something to meet our client's needs on a frequent basis. They deserve a lot of attention as one of our most valuable assets. Preparing for the future takes concentrated effort.

Competing Creatively for the Future (A Practical Exercise)

1. Identify your four major competitors.
2. Have four teams play the role of one competitor each and describe their 3- and 5-year plans.
3. Review the four competitive plans and think through your company's best Plan A and Plan B.
4. Imagine two new competitors not in the original four and what their best 3- and 5-year plans would be.
5. Now, refine your best Plan A to A* and Plan B to B* and add a Plan C*.
6. Identify the key assumptions, resources, and so on, in Plans A*, B* and C* and think through the most reason-

able alternative to follow consistent with your company mission.

7. Challenge the thinking again in a year. Confirm or redefine the company mission, for clarity, every three years.

Miracles are instantaneous, they cannot be summoned, they come of themselves, usually at the unlikely moments and to those who least expect them.

Katherine Anne Porter

The president said it would be very helpful if he had a list of all the ways that we now gather information and turn it into Market Intelligence by a thorough analysis.

16

Market Intelligence

Information gathered and carefully analyzed can lead to Market Intelligence, which is extremely valuable as a business staff plans its strategies and tactics.

Joe Chameleon returned from a top management meeting on Wednesday and said to Frank Cloud, his R & D associate, "I heard the strangest request today. Our president said it would be very helpful if he had a list of all the ways that we now gather information and turn it into Market Intelligence by a thorough analysis. What do you think of that, Frank?" Frank winced a bit and then said, "That's a reasonable question. I have some ideas to contribute to the list, but let's also include Mary Lou Smartken. With her MBA and PhD in marketing, she should be able to help significantly." "Good thinking, Frank. I'll arrange a meeting for Monday or Tuesday, so we can impress the boss that we are on our toes and have the answers for him at next Wednesday's meeting." "A good analysis will take a lot more than one meeting," said Frank. "Sorry, it has to be done by next Wednesday," maintained Joe.

Mary Lou was happy to participate in the thinking and preferred to give the report herself. However, Joe finally convinced Frank and Mary Lou that he would make the presentation and they would be in attendance at the back of the room. What Mary Lou and Frank didn't know was that Joe had already bragged to the president, "No problem, I'll put that together for you for next Wednesday."

"Let's start off by making a list in different categories," said Mary Lou. "You know, types of information needed, sources of information, types of analysis needed and associates who can assist in analysis." "Good start. And what do you think, Frank?" asked Joe. Frank pondered and commented, "My product research is what I could see being influenced by Market Intelligence. We should categorize the information gathering into its long-range and short-term impact on our decisions."

After two hours of give and take, Joe summarized the conclusions as follows:

Six Information Sources Within Our Company	Ways Of Tapping	Six Information Sources Outside Our Company	Ways Of Tapping
Associates	Gather their knowledge on the needs of clients, the offerings of competitors, and their view of industry trends.	Candidates for hire	Talk to them extensively about their experiences with your competitors where they have worked.
Company sales data	Excellent source of information on client purchase trends by product, by salesperson, by price point.	Vendors	Listen carefully to their stories of industry trends and actions of our competitors.
Client satisfaction levels	Routine part of marketing department surveys.	Trade journals	Industry interviews, statistics on market-share, and so on.

Six Information Sources Within Our Company	Ways Of Tapping	Six Information Sources Outside Our Company	Ways Of Tapping
Analysis of clients' needs for new products or services	Focus groups, concept studies, telephone surveys, personal interviews, sales staff feedback.	Competitions' public press releases, annual reports, 10K's, quarterly reports, and so on.	Someone in our company owns a few shares in each major competitor or obtains from a stockbroker.
Position of our company in the minds of clients and prospects	Polling approaches, image studies or questionnaires, advertising research.	Financial analysts' reports of companies and the industry	Library, internet, stock brokers.
Product performance data	Quality control records and analysis of products as shipped. Complaint records.	Interests of competitors outside of business (United Way, hospital, breast cancer research, and so on.)	Local newspaper of the city where competitors' CEO lives. (Note: Particularly useful in acquisition intelligence collection – personal side)

"That's enough," said Joe Chameleon. "Twelve approaches will convince the president that we are on top of our jobs." "But wait," said Mary Lou. "That's only the start. We need to identify the key management decisions that these types of Market Intelligence will influence." "I agree," said Frank. "We just scratched the surface." "Sorry," said Joe, "I've got to go to my next meeting now, and I'm convinced this will satisfy the president." "Where does the president really want to go with this line of thought?" asked Mary Lou. "I haven't got a clue," said Joe, "but we'll all find out at 10:30 on Wednesday."

Some frustration existed on the part of Mary Lou and Frank, and yet a start was made on an important line of thinking. Joe may be manipulating them for his personal benefit, but at least they have a small sense of having contributed.

The outcome will depend on the reaction of the president on Wednesday.

How is the subject of Market Intelligence handled in your business? Is it important? Does it get the proper attention?

And stand together, yet not too near together. For the pillars of the temple stand apart, and the oak tree and cypress grow not in each other's shadow.

Kahlil Gibran

Creative Corporate Culture

The use of champions, teams, special task forces or ad hoc groups to address a specific challenge are some of the ways to encourage people to rally around a business objective.

17

Our Business

The corner grocery store owner knows who is in charge of all decisions, success and failure. She is the owner and the only associate. As businesses grow and add associates, it is critical that the associates see the business as "our business."

Entrepreneurs take risks. Like Barbara Chen, they often put twice as many hours per week into their job as most associates. They are emotionally involved in the business they are leading. They may be considered workaholics, like Barbara. Seven days a week and twelve hours a day, they are thinking about their business. They want it to succeed so much that they hurt inside emotionally and physically when the business takes a bad turn. They are fantastically exuberant when the business has some success, however small. Entrepreneurs like Barbara thoroughly enjoy their work.

Ralph Rodriguez was a nine to five worker. For him the job was just a job. He didn't have any picture in his mind of his job being an important part of the business. Nights and weekends were for pleasurable activities—certainly not work. Barbara and Ralph, by chance, ended up working together on the same new product project. Initially management felt, "We have to use Ralph for something. He can't hurt the project too badly. Barbara will carry it in any case." Ralph felt, "I'll put in my time and we'll see what happens. At least this job might be something new—not quite so boring." Barbara felt, "What on earth did I do to cause management to put Ralph on this project with me? He's going to be a drag. Every time a new approach comes up, he's negative. This is not what I had hoped for on the new product team."

After two months (nothing happens overnight), Ralph was excited about the new product. Ralph and Barbara had divided up the tasks and set an aggressive timetable to bring it to commercialization. This was their product. This was going to be their business. They had a personal involvement; "our business" was the way they described it. When the business succeeded, they were thrilled. When the business had a downturn, they worked extra hard to get more business. Two factors had changed Ralph's attitude—Barbara's drive and enthusiasm and his own innate desire to do something of importance.

How many Ralphs and Barbaras have you managed? Have you coached them to think of the business as "our business?" A job takes on a whole new excitement when you picture it in your mind as needing you personally and only being successful with your unique contribution.

By their nature, small family-owned businesses have an opportunity to develop very strong bonds of teamwork and esprit de corps. But it is critical that the business owner, or the family leader, convey a family atmosphere, a teamwork atmosphere, an atmosphere of the business being "our business." Stock ownership and profit sharing plans have been found to be very strong motivators to help associates become very concerned about the health of the business. Money alone may not be the strongest motivator, but it certainly provides an excellent feedback system when your hard work leads to business success, which leads to a substantial increase in the value of your stock or in your profit sharing income.

In coming years, various forms of profit sharing among associates will likely grow in use in all types of business. Of course, the difficult area is loss sharing. In a bad year, if the associates' income is less than in a good business year, then a true incentive system for improved effectiveness has been established. "Our business" means "our business," in good times and bad.

The use of champions, teams, special task forces or ad hoc groups to address a specific challenge are some of the ways to encourage people to rally around a business objective. Charlie Simpson had a unique solution to a difficult research problem. He had two ways to technologically produce a product, but he was not sure which was the best solution when manufacturing cost and product desirability to the clients were taken into consideration. Charlie formed two teams, and each group was given all the research, manufacturing and marketing expertise to pilot the product. Instead of taking the traditional two years to get to market, he challenged both teams to aim for introduction in ten months. The ground rules were clear, and everyone involved knew that only one technological route would finally be commercialized. During those ten months, the two teams owned the challenge. They worked as competing teams but shared all their findings with each other, for after all, the real competitors were outside the company. They worked day and night, weekdays and weekends for ten months. They celebrated at the end. One team had demonstrated the best product for the market. The other team had developed the second best product for the market, far superior in cost and performance to competitors outside of the company. For at least this ten-month period, those team members owned the business just as truly as if they had the stock in their safe-deposit boxes.

Charlie Simpson was a creative business leader. People liked to work for Charlie. He set tough challenges and joined everyone in trying to meet them. On Thursday evening, Saturday morning, and Sunday afternoon, Charlie was there encouraging the two teams. Charlie was an inspirational leader who knew the value of being a visible leader.

Sometimes it is important to share financial information quite broadly in a business if the goal is to have a broad cross section of the associates feel as though they can call it "our business." Business has certain yardsticks, such as sales, expenses, pretax earnings, return on investment and cash flow. Management needs to make a very conscious decision on how much financial information to share and how broadly. Different corporate cultures set different boundaries. However large or small, a business leader needs to decide how much information to trust his or her associates with. The risks are real when sensitive information is shared. The potential benefits are also real when associates know the yardsticks, and are working in a concerted creative effort to meet the yardsticks. They like to know how their job affects the numbers.

In developing a concept of "our business" in an organization, a spirit of entrepreneurship needs to be balanced with a measured dose of open communication on business success criteria.

Two things fill my mind with ever new and increasing wonder and awe; the starry heavens above me and the moral law within me.
Immanuel Kant

People live up to their expectations of themselves. Their expectations of themselves are greatly influenced by the positive reinforcement they receive from their manager.

18

Positive Reinforcement

How many times last year did your manager point out to you where you had done a very good job? How many times last year did your manager point out a mistake or a poor job? What ratio of positive to negative comments do you confer on your associates? Are you pleased with that ratio? Is it the most effective way to get the best job done?

Dale Carnegie created a hugely successful business that has made a great contribution to millions of people based on the premise of positive thinking and positive reinforcement. Norman Vincent Peele's book, *The Power of Positive Thinking,* was the beginning of literally hundreds of books on a positive approach to life. And going way back, we have the golden rule—do unto others as you would have them do unto you.

We know, but how often do we use, the powerful technique of positive reinforcement? There are literally thousands of opportunities every year that we miss the golden opportunities to praise someone. One popular phrase, "catch someone doing something right," is a reminder that we as managers so often are critical and so seldom are using positive reinforcement.

Yet, we forget and miss those golden opportunities. As managers, we focus a great deal on the exceptions and call it management by exception. We are so busy that we feel we need to reserve ourselves for the problems. Well, the principles of positive reinforcement suggest that if we focus on the good results, our organization will have those good results in their minds and will accomplish more good results. People live up to their expectations of themselves. Their expectations of themselves are greatly influenced by the positive reinforcement they receive from their manager.

We have all had associates who have achieved goals beyond what they and we would have imagined. Tricia Anderson was such an associate. She "knew" she was very shy. She "knew" she wasn't creative. She perceived herself as a plodder, not an innovator. Her manager, Joe Quirk, tried everything he could imagine to help her grow, to think more of her strengths. Positive reinforcement was the key. Tricia would say, "That isn't my style, to give a presentation to 100 people. I just can't see myself doing it." Joe would say, "Let's try it on a small group of six people, then you will know it so well that you can just give the presentation to six people in the audience, while the 94 others just happen to be there." Tricia would say, "Creating a brand new sales program is certainly not what I expected to do when I graduated from college." Joe would say, "Talk to a few salespeople. Get their ideas. Test those ideas on a few other salespeople. Add an idea or two of your own. Then let's talk about how a total sales program might look." Tricia grew from Joe's coaching.

Are you using the positive reinforcement skills that Joe

Quirk found so successful? Or are you practicing exception management and focusing much more time on correction and criticism than you are on praise?

Psychologically, we all strive for positive reinforcement. We avoid criticism. We get defensive if we are corrected. Suppose, just suppose, that we praised our associates ten times for every time we criticized them. Wouldn't they accept the criticism in a much less defensive manner?

Do unto others as you would have them do unto you. Reinforce positively; perhaps even your manager would like to read this chapter. Positive reinforcement is not just a warm, fuzzy approach to management. It is a time-tested formula for a more effective way to get the best job done. It is a cornerstone of a dynamic, successful business, and it makes the business world more fun and more humane.

There is more hunger for love and appreciation in this world than for bread.
Mother Theresa

An effective manager is very quick with dispensing credit to an individual or a group effort but very slow to assign blame.

19

Credit and Blame

It is amazing how much can be accomplished when you are not worried about who will get the credit or blame.

The business world is full of the competitive spirit. We try to invent better products and services than our competitors and satisfy the clients better and increase our company's share of the market opportunity. Competition is healthy; it brings out the best and gives the clients more choices. Competition among companies is a critically important part of the free enterprise system.

So isn't it natural to encourage competition among associates within a corporation? Let the best person win. Show us what you can do. Which of you will be the top performer this year? The next promotion will go to the best performer. How have you contributed in the past year that distinguished you from your peers?

We all have been involved in public discussions of challenge and private discussions of performance. Sometimes we have been happy with the results of such encounters, and often we have been disappointed.

Perhaps the answer revolves around the words "teamwork," "credit" and "blame." Let's consider the situation of Ronald Blackwell. You may have had a manager like him during your career. And, perhaps, if you see some of yourself in him, it is appropriate to ask yourself, "Could we accomplish more if I wasn't worried about who will get the credit or blame?" Ronald was a middle manager with several levels of management reporting to him; he managed other managers. Ronald was a master at telling upper members of management what he thought they wanted to hear. If they asked, "Did Joe check on the delivery schedule to be sure we wouldn't get into this mess?" Ronald, who had Joe's boss Mary reporting directly to him, would often say, "You have a good point. Maybe Joe didn't check enough. I'll have Mary get a report to you on the delivery schedule by Friday." Ronald was always quick to sidestep his part of the responsibility for managing the business and quick to imply that someone in his organization had goofed. He was often assigning blame before he knew all the facts. How many Ronald Blackwells have you worked for in the past?

Ronald was always responsive to management. He responded to their requests quickly by passing jobs down the line. Sometimes months or years later people in the organization would find that they had been found guilty in the eyes of top management without all the evidence, or almost any of the evidence, being sought.

Oh yes, when Ronald found that Joe had done an outstanding job and Mary had paid close attention to her management responsibilities, Ronald was very reluctant to pass those findings on to top management. He had created an image about one of his associates and to admit that he was wrong would be to decrease his credibility with top management. Ronald was out for himself. Credit, he was happy to accept; blame, he was happy to pass on to his subordinates. How many Ronald Blackwells do you know? Too many, right?

In contrast, let's take the example of Ann Olsen. Ann had a job similar in responsibility to Ronald, but she had a dramatically different philosophy toward her associates. When her boss would ask her, "Did Joe check on the delivery schedule to be sure we would not get into this mess?" Mary would quickly recognize it as the beginning of a blame hunt. Her response frequently would be something like; "Joe and Mary have been working very creatively on the delivery schedule for months. We are running 98 percent accuracy, so I'm sure there is a good explanation for the current mess. I will give you a verbal update this afternoon." Ann would always present her associates in a positive light, and they appreciated it. They worked very hard and very creatively because they knew that Ann would always work with them as a team. Ann would acknowledge her personal responsibility in her management task. Most people like to work for Ann Olsens and dislike working for Ronald Blackwells.

Associates enjoy the pat on the back and fully recognize when they goof. An effective manager is very quick with dispensing credit to an individual or a group effort but very slow to assign blame. Yes, sometimes individuals need to be put on probation, and sometimes individuals need to be fired. But, generally, in most of our business transactions, we can get more accomplished by not worrying about who will get the credit or blame. The focus is best placed on getting the job done effectively as a team.

Finally, instead of credit and blame, consider the concepts of continuous improvement of business methods—every day and every week. By analysis, the root cause of problems can be identified so that the business methods can be improved. With improved business methods, all associates have a better chance at successful outcomes.

Every experience in life is a chisel which has been cutting away at our life statue, molding and shaping it. We are part of all we have met.
Orison Swett Marden

20

Flexible and Feasible

"I work for a flexible company. What you requested could be feasible. Let's talk some more."

These are powerful words, and a powerful thought is behind them. When talking with clients and prospects, these words keep a conversation open instead of reacting with statements which put barriers up for the clients. Lynda Listener was excellent at this approach. I asked her one day, "How did you find out that flexible and feasible was so useful with clients?" "Well," she related, "for five years I was using my standard approach, and when a client would come off the wall with a question like, 'Why can't I get a 20 percent discount?' I felt very defensive." "Tell me about it," I said. Lynda continued, "My usual reaction was polite but firm. I'd say something like, 'I wish I could give you the 20 percent discount, but our company just doesn't have a policy to do that.' Then I would find the clients saying, 'I'm not too interested in your product unless you can give me the 20 percent discount that I get from your competitors. Whenever I used the word policy or standard program or authorized offer, it got the client upset. Then, one manager I had suggested I handle these situations differently. Instead of closing out the client with essentially a 'can't do it' statement, I used my new statement to keep the conversation open: 'I work for a flexible company. What you requested could be feasible. Let's talk some more.' It works like a charm!!'"

Often the client goes on to explain more about why he wants a better discount, faster delivery, a new product and what basis he is using to justify the request. It is strange how a $100,000 order can be delivered this week, even if I have to deliver it in my own personal car. A lot of things are feasible when the request is clear and some creativity is applied to work out a solution. Asking probing questions is critical in uncovering an approach to solving the client's problems: "Would it help if…." By posing alternative solutions, it is usually possible to reach a workable solution for both parties. "Call it creative negotiation if you will," said Lynda. "I call it my flexible/feasible statement, and I say it just the same every time. It works, so I use it."

I tested the concept in one of our factories with one of the engineers. "Joe," I said, "we really need this new product in six months to keep up with competition." I expected him to say, "No way José. You know it takes two years to develop a product like that. The best we have ever done is 21 months." But what he really said was, "You and I work for a flexible company. Six months might be feasible; let's talk some more." I was delighted to see this open attitude from a person in engineering. When we talked further, we both understood the need better. Normally, the specifications on a new product are so difficult and so firm that it takes 21 to 24 months to meet them. Joe pointed out that two specifications were really the tough ones. I found out that those could be relaxed somewhat and Joe then felt this was a much easier project and four to six months could be counted on. Keeping the communications open had helped us jointly reach a good solution.

Then I talked to one of the night foremen. "Fred," I said, "I need 50 percent blue and 50 percent white next month. I'm sorry I previously told you 80 percent/20 percent but the clients are buying more white than I had anticipated." I expected Fred to go into orbit for changing my needs on such short notice. He said, "We both work for a flexible company, and that means it is feasible for me to make some changes in my production schedule. Would it be possible to deliver mostly blue in the beginning of the month and catch up on the white, so by the end of the month I've reached your 50/50 need?" "Sure," I said, "it's only the full month that we have to balance at 50/50, not every week. Flexible and feasible, open communication, negotiating to a win-win situation—whatever you call it, it's powerful.

Lynda Listener had had a good manager as a coach. Fortunately, the business is better off because the flexible/feasible concept is helping all communications throughout the company.

The future belongs to those who believe in the beauty of their dreams.
Eleanor Roosevelt

The purpose of any meeting is the transfer of meaning from some people's minds to others. It pays to be as creative as possible in the techniques you employ to get a meeting of the minds.

21

Meeting of the Minds

The atmosphere of a meeting is strongly influenced by the physical environment and the manner in which the meeting is conducted. Too often we limit the potential of getting people together by lack of attention to the meeting atmosphere. Associates spend a great deal of their time in meetings so it makes sense to talk about the most effective use of that valuable time. Meetings have many purposes, so they should take many forms.

Hallway Meetings

Probably the most useful of all meetings, when measured for effectiveness per time spent, is the hallway meeting.

"Hi, Joe, I was thinking about you this morning. Would it be possible to move the entrance to the shipping department to the east side of the plant? That would give us some more room for expansion of the new product area." "Sure, Fred. That's a possibility. We could also make room for the new product area on the north side of shipping. Would it be convenient for me to stop by your office this afternoon about 2:00 p.m. to show you some options my associates have developed?" "Sounds good, but I have a conflict at 2:00 p.m. Could we do it at 3:00 p.m.?" "Sure, see you then." A lot of information has been conveyed, two ways, in a very short time. This stand up, hallway meeting has helped both parties get closer to their objectives and helped the business become more successful.

"But," says the associate, "I can't always count on just meeting people in the hallway." Yes you can—effectively. George Rifle was a master at hallway meetings. He almost always walked around the plant, or the sales, laboratory or administrative offices with his mind set on four or five people he wanted to talk to briefly about key subjects. He had found three minute face-to-face meetings to be extremely effective after years of experience. George would take several pieces of paper on selected subjects with him as he walked the hallways. In a normal hour he would have contacted at least two of the people he wanted to see and frequently five or six others. Some conversations were sociable, "I heard you went to the beach this weekend; it sure was perfect weather for it. You have a place at the beach, don't you?" Some hallway meetings were to congratulate people. "Anne, Frank told me about your three new sales last week. That's terrific. I'm sure you were pleased to complete those three agreements. I want you to know we really appreciate your hard work and your creative approach to your job." George Rifle was a pro. He would find someone at their desk and ask, "Have you got just a minute?" Then, out of his ever present folder would come a page he wanted to discuss. He'd sit on the edge of the desk, not in a chair. "Mary," George would say, "these numbers don't seem to explain our earnings problems. Was there something unusual that happened in May?" "Sure," Mary Specifico would say. "We had a write-off in May of some obsolete inventory. I guess I should have put it in the report as a footnote." "Well, now I remember the write-off. That explains the low numbers. Thanks, Mary. I know I can count on you to explain things. See you at the business review meeting tomorrow." Mary then volunteered, "Oh, I meant to tell you, George, at the meeting tomorrow I am going to urge that we purchase a new computer. I hope I can count on your support." George gulped, "Is this the big $50,000 model or the $15,000 model?" Mary smiled, "We have found ways to make the $15,000 model do our job." "Good," said George. "I'll support you 100 percent." George was a professional at hallway meetings and, by his example, people such as Mary were learning how to communicate important subjects quickly and effectively to reach a meeting of the minds with another individual.

New Possibilities Meetings

There are occasions when a manager wants to get a group of people to think some new creative thoughts. George Rifle loved these meetings. Some called them brainstorming meetings, others called them think-tank sessions, but in any case, they were important to the health of the business. The ideas and new possibilities generated in these meetings often could be found in routine use several months later. "Creative meetings like these need a creative atmosphere," George would describe from his experience. "People are more creative when the atmosphere is informal and relaxed. People all dressed up in a standard conference room just don't, on average, come out with as many real, creative ideas. I've found that a relaxed atmosphere often leads to the best creative ideas. The relaxed dress and atmosphere also breaks down any barriers created by the corporate pecking order. When everyone is wearing blue jeans and is working around a round table away from the office phone, a wild, creative idea has more chance of being fairly considered than it would be in a formal presentation setting in headquarters with the your general manager at the head of the table." George explained further, "I tried to explain that to our Board of Directors. I don't believe they would feel comfortable if they didn't meet in the same room all the time with the same seats around the same long, narrow table. I honestly believe our Board of Directors is limiting their creative thinking by the atmosphere they have created for themselves. Twice I've seen them try the informal atmosphere I suggested—not quite blue jeans but at least sports shirts at a conference center. Both times, some really new ideas were generated. But they have returned to the security and emotional comfort of the Board Room."

The Powerful Chart Pad

George Rifle always insisted that his office had two large chart pads on the wall and that meetings had two large easels with chart pads on them. George explained his philosophy of the powerful chart pad: "I try to have people form a horseshoe around my round table facing the chart pads. The chart pads provide a great psychological tool for the meeting participants. We can generate ideas and put them on the charts. We are all facing the charts so it is like we are facing the problem or opportunity together. It generates an atmosphere of teamwork. Once an idea is up on the chart, that person doesn't have the psychological need to protect and defend it. If no one supports his idea, he can forget it without losing face (as contrasted to people sitting across from each other defending each idea in an apparent win/lose situation).

When several people rally around one of the ideas which were generated, it develops an atmosphere of teamwork without the originator of the idea having to boast that it was her idea. The power of the chart pad is that it helps people save face and helps people generate team solutions to problems."

George continued, "In a bigger meeting, the chart pad serves as a great way to record conclusions. Suppose we are progressing through a meeting and a decision is made. It is extremely useful to chart that decision, be sure everyone agrees to it, and then proceed with the discussion of other issues. It is amazing how conversations are kept on the subject by this technique. Decisions and agreements are recorded. If some follow-up steps are needed, that is charted also. We could call this approach 'public consensus' or 'meeting minutes during the meeting'."

We've used chart pads to draw pictures also. It is a powerful tool! A picture really communicates more than a thousand words. One manager when asked to draw a picture of how he felt in the business, drew a sketch of himself with hands above his head holding a big box with the label on it THE BUSINESS. He described his picture by saying he felt like he was holding up the business all by himself and that it was a difficult, awesome responsibility. The other participants in the session volunteered that they would love to help if he would just delegate some responsibility to them and share more information with them. It was like a magic wand had passed over the room. The general manager and his managers had opened a dialog that just would not have happened in a normal meeting. The chart pad and the picture has been a vivid image in everyone's mind who attended that meeting. The management team began at that point to work more as an effective management team. Pecking order was not as important as what the business needed and what each person could contribute."

"Ask people to draw a picture of their vision of the future of your business and you will find some fascinating things," said George. "Some will draw a ship halfway under the water, others will draw a jungle with dozens of animals fighting over one piece of meat, others will draw a sunset, others will draw a sunrise. Then, the conversation about the reasons each person drew their picture leads to an outstanding understanding of each person's real feelings about the business and its future. By contrasting where we envision the business to be headed and where we would like to see it headed, we can develop a plan for getting it to the desired end state. Pictures and chart pads help this planning process."

Sam Critique interrupted George, "George, I just don't buy what you have been saying. You make us out to be soft headed weaklings who can't handle a business situation unless you put us through a special process of meeting management.

I think you got hooked on this atmosphere baloney and now are touting it as the solution to all problems. I prefer more conventional meetings where I know where I stand and there are no big surprises. I can defend my organization's performance just as well that way you call old-fashioned, and save the company a lot of money by not having to go offsite to a special conference center." "I get your point, Sam. The meeting atmosphere should help a group of people work on a problem or a possibility and should not get in the way. In fact, our experience shows that the best approach to planning a special meeting is to have a few people who will be attending the meeting carefully address the question of where, how long, what agenda, who leads what portions, how introduced and how concluded." Sam impatiently interrupted, "Now you are suggesting meetings to plan for meetings. Talk about overkill." George responded, "Have you ever attended a meeting that you felt could have been more effective? Sure you have, Sam. And I will bet you generally felt that if someone had just asked you, you could have given them some good advice on how to run the meeting." "Okay, I'll agree to that," said Sam. "Well then, some thought by a few of the participants for a meeting can be helpful in planning it. Sure, I agree, more planning is needed for big meetings but a few minutes spent by a few people planning for a one-hour meeting might make it as effective as a two-hour meeting." Sam suggested, "Okay, I'm sold. Please have some orange magic markers for me to write my ideas on the chart pads. I am not afraid to have my ideas stand out."

Every organization has a Sam Critique and they can be

valuable contributors. However, with more than one Sam Critique on a staff, you may want to consider different steps than meeting design to engender teamwork.

Other Meeting-of-the-Minds Concepts

♦ Try to avoid meetings that do not lead to decisions. If the meeting is for the dissemination of information, can it be done more effectively by just distributing the information by E-mail?

♦ Encourage short meetings. A lot can be covered in 30 minutes. If two hours are scheduled, people will feel obligated to fill the two hours.

♦ Keep the number of people involved in each meeting to the point where each is expected to contribute. All meeting attendees should be expected to be meeting contributors.

♦ Strongly encourage hallway meetings as a technique for avoiding longer meetings.

♦ When a major subject needs to be discussed, treat it accordingly. Give it all the time it needs without interruption. Don't spend two hours debating the color for the bathroom doors and ten minutes deciding on a $2 million business expansion proposal. (Oh, how many times we have all witnessed this happen. Why don't we try to change it to a more effective time versus importance proportion?)

Meeting of the Minds Overview

As George Rifle has explained to us, "The purpose of

any meeting is the transfer of meaning from some people's minds to others. The transfer of meaning and the dialog that involves is critical to effective communication and the effective management of a business. It pays to be as creative as possible in the techniques you employ to get a meeting of the minds."

People want riches. They need fulfillment.
Bob Conklin

The excitement of working in a flat pyramid structure is real. True bureaucrats love tall, thin, complex organization structures loaded with staff assistants. Really effective business leaders love flat pyramids.

22

The Flat Organizational Pyramid

Hierarchies tend to grow to the point where more creative energy is spent on preserving and growing the hierarchy than is spent on meeting the goals of serving clients and rewarding investors.

Symptoms of the organization pyramid not being flat enough:

- Lots of corridor conversation on who is going to get the job that Sam left last week. (No conversation on whether the job could be done just as well some other way without replacing him.)

- Many sign-off sheets with five to ten people attesting to the approval of a project with a signature. (No one questioning whether some additional delegation of authority might be useful for business effectiveness.)

- Many people who have only one, two or three people reporting to them. (Managers with three or fewer people reporting to them are not doing a number of the projects independently as a contributor supplementing the work of their few associates.)

- Individuals in the organization who feel they lack scope in their job. (Jobs which are very narrowly defined.)

- Managers with an entrepreneurial spirit leaving the company. (Hierarchies with plenty of rules to slow down any individual with creative flair.)
- Procedure manuals.
- Job descriptions in detail. (Little room for the individual to change the nature of his job over time.)
- Difficulty in getting decisions made. (Many people need to be involved and it takes weeks to even get the first meeting scheduled to review the subject.)
- Meetings that lead to more meetings, not decisions.
- Many staff assistants in the organization chart.

There are many recognized needs for an organizational structure to help a company administer its business. But the structure can become a burden rather than a help if it is too tall and thin. A flat organizational pyramid has several key advantages:

1. Each individual has a broader responsibility so must be creative in fulfilling those responsibilities. Each individual must enrich his contribution to his own job. Therefore, associates will be coming closer to using their full potential. Delegation of responsibility will be more prevalent.

2. Managers will focus on the overview of managing rather than the detail of doing. The strategies and directions for efforts will be more focused because of the manager's broader view of the business to empower the clients.

3. Costs will be lower. Few managers are needed when each has eight or ten associates reporting to them rather than three or four.

4. Decisions will be more timely to meet the needs of the clients.

As experienced managers, we all recognize the informal organization as extremely valuable in getting the job done. Often, the formal organizational diagram is put aside to get a job done more effectively. A task force is formed with associates from several organizations. Some are young and low on the formal organization chart. Some are quite experienced. Together they represent a mix of knowledge to get a task done effectively. Flexibility is essential.

Consider the job of staff assistant. Margaret Stuart was a staff assistant par excellence. Her boss was a production manager. When her manager wanted details from the plants, he would ask Margaret to get them for him. Margaret would work with many people in the several plants, gather all the details, and summarize them for her manager and then go on to the next information-gathering project. Maybe that sounds good to you—the manager has received the information he wanted and has not had to spend a lot of his own time.

What happened before Margaret Stuart was assigned? The boss would ask his plant managers for these details. Their first reaction was always, "Come on boss, do you really need to know that—my organization has that under control." But when the boss insisted, the plant managers would get the information assembled. Then, Margaret Stuart was assigned. Would you think the plant managers would be happy or upset? They were very upset. Margaret consistently went around them and got the information the boss wanted from area supervisors and engineers in the plant. On many issues, the production manager was better informed on the details than the plant managers were and he reminded them of specific situations periodically.

The production manager had a great desire to manage the details, and Margaret helped him get around the reluctant plant managers. Important staff versus line relationships and questions develop. Margaret was likable but was not too well liked by the plant managers. The production manager needed the details...or did he? That is a big question. When staff assistants are being considered, we should ask, "Can I not get the information I really need to conduct my business from my line organization? Why not? Am I delegating enough to my line organization or am I doing part of their job for them? Can these questions be handled by the line organization with their existing staffs?" Staff assistants can be very valuable or they can be a sign of a problem with a pyramid that is not flat enough. It is worth worrying about.

How many people process a piece of information in your organization before a decision is made? For example, sales for the first half of the month are not up to the expected level. In a flat pyramid structure, action should be taken at the first or second level to bolster efforts to improve sales. In tall, thin pyramid structures the information may not even be available at the first and second level. Middle and top management and many home office analysts speculate on what is happening to sales—the economy, the competition, our back orders, and so on. Meetings are held. Five different groups speculate on the situation but no one takes an action to bolster sales for months. Does something like this ever happen in your business? Are you spending more creative energy inside the business talking to each other about what the problem might be and why our estimate this week is different than our estimate last week then you are spending energy on stimulating sales for the next two weeks? Sometimes pyramids that are not flat enough spend a lot of time processing information, having meetings, sending letters, and administering the organization. Flat pyramid organizations get on with it; they make decisions and take action.

So the flat pyramid has several key advantages. The excitement of working in a flat pyramid structure is real. True bureaucrats love tall, thin, complex organization structures loaded with staff assistants. Really effective business leaders love flat pyramids. Have you looked at your pyramid lately? Chances are it is not as flat as you may want it to be to have your organization be very effective in the marketplace and empowering your clients and very effective internally with motivated, creative associates.

Costs, Morale and the Organizational Pyramid

Let's take a simplified example where 10,000 first line people are needed. With one manager for ten, that would require 1,000 first line managers. To manage the managers and continue with the one for ten ratio would require 100 middle managers, and so on, with the top management level of 10 and one CEO. The total is 11,111 associates with 10,000 first line people. Ten thousand out of 11,111 represents a 90 percent efficiency and a CEO with only four other job levels in an organization of 11,111.

Experienced managers are aware that it is sometimes challenging to manage ten others, but it can be done with good delegation, training, and alignment toward a common vision.

How close is your organization to the 90 percent efficiency goal? 40 percent? 50 percent? 60 percent? Would you suspect that your business' effectiveness in the marketplace would improve as you approach the 90 percent efficiency level?

We suggest that everyone would find such an organization very effective with paperwork and bureaucracy greatly reduced, communications outstanding, and all associates empowered to empower the clients.

Suppose each level in the organization were paid double the lower level. For example:

First line associates=10,000 @	$20,000 each=	$200,000,000
First line management=1,000 @	$40,000 each=	$40,000,000
Middle management=100 @	$80,000 each=	$8,000,000
Top management =10 @	$160,000 each=	$1,600,000
CEO=1 @	$320,000 each=	$320,000
Total number of associates: 11,111=		$249,920,000
AVERAGE PAY = $22,500 EACH		

(Over 80 percent of all salaries and wages for first line associates.)

How does the pay pattern for this organization ($22,500 average vs. $20,000 for the first line associates) compare with your organization? Where do you want your organization to be? How can you get there? Will the benefit be empowered associates in addition to cost reduction? (I submit that the empowered associates will probably be the most important long-term benefit because they empower the clients.)

Keep love in your heart. A life without love is like a scentless garden when the flowers are dead.
Oscar Wilde

By not adequately communicating probabilities of achieving a forecast, the different members of management are operating with different yardsticks for measuring performance.

23

Forecasting

Forecasting would be easy if we didn't have to deal with uncertainties and the future.

In our business world, we are frequently working with forecasts. How are our sales in the Western Region versus our forecast? How are our expenses versus forecast in the Illinois plant? Is our new product introduction timetable on forecast? Why are we running at twice the quality reject level that we forecast? Why is the engineering prototype three months behind forecast? And, oh yes, how do you explain being so far ahead of the earnings forecast through March? Was our forecast not challenging enough when we made it?

There are many techniques for forecasting—analyzing past experiences and estimating what will happen during the next period, computer simulation, back of the envelope guessing, top down forecasts that top management says we need to meet, bottom up forecasts that people close to the day-to-day activities feel are reasonable.

Many hours are spent preparing forecasts, and many hours are spent during a year comparing actual performance versus a forecast. Is it all useful or not? Where would we be if we did not make forecasts: just compare versus the previous year? Would that be a better approach?

Forecasting and planning are two inseparable concepts. If a sales forecast is for 5 percent per year volume growth, a plant expansion program does not have to be as aggressive as if the sales forecast is for 50 percent per year volume growth. Will the 5 percent or the 50 percent forecast both likely be wrong? Yes, no forecast is perfect. But the plant capacity often needs to be planned one, two or three years before it is needed for meeting client's orders. So some form of forecasting is important. A business needs to be quite accurate in projecting its future in broad terms. Are we going to grow rapidly or slowly, shrink slowly or rapidly?

That seems simple—rapid or slow growth, rapid or slow decline. However, if a business or a product line or a market segment can at least be put into one of the four categories, no major business mistakes will be made. Careful analysis of the markets, the environment, the competitors, our products, our service and our skills are necessary to decide which of the four categories each of our businesses is in.

Forecasts often are done for financial planning purposes; controllers and accountants frequently insist on a great deal of detail. Every business needs to define how much detail is needed, but as a general principle, forecast making and actual versus forecast auditing should be focused on decision-making needs. Jeremy Nason was one of the best managers I know at clarifying the role of forecasts and cutting down on the unnecessary detail. Jeremy continually asked, "What actions will be taken as a result of this review of actual versus forecast performance?" Frequently, people answered, "The next higher level in the organization needs it." Jeremy would then ask the next higher level managers. They would say their bosses or their subordinates needed the analysis and made action-oriented decisions based on it. Jeremy found that many forecasts and comparisons versus forecasts were done only because they were done the previous year. Reports and procedures tend to be institutionalized to the point that no one questions them but no one is taking actions based on them. Jeremy was tenacious in eliminating all forecasts that had no owners who were using them to make decisions. Do you have a Jeremy in your organization? Are you willing to help a Jeremy do his job?

Forecasts are funny things. They are often dramatically misunderstood. For an example, let's analyze a manufacturing cost forecast. During the previous year the manufacturing cost at a certain company was $2,200 per unit with 3,000 units produced for sale. In other words, the total manufacturing cost was $6,600,000. Now it is forecast time and management asks the manufacturing manager to make his cost forecast for the coming year. The conversation often goes like this (greatly condensed, of course):

Top Manager (Sarah Edison)

"Bill, you got the cost down to $2,200 per unit last year. It would be great if you could reach $1,800 per unit this year. How about we forecast $1,800 per unit?"

Manufacturing Manager (Bill Schwartz)

"Sarah, you understand that we got a great break on our raw materials last year. This year our parts vendors have told us prices will go up about 6 percent. And, of course, our labor contract also calls for a 3 percent wage increase this year. But to top it all off, our sales organization has told me we only expect to sell 2,500 units this year so my production task is down from 3,000 to 2,500 units. With the higher parts prices, higher wages, and less units to absorb our overhead expenses, I'd expect our cost to go up to $2,500 per unit."

Note: The boundaries are now set. The forecast will be somewhere between $1,800 and $2,500 per unit.

Top Manager (Sarah Edison)

"Bill, I understand your point of view but we just need a lower cost. Then our sales people can give a few discounts and we will have a better chance of selling 3,000 or even more units. Can't you figure some way to save several hundred dollars per unit? We can't submit a forecast to corporate management (said with strong emphasis) that has an increase in manufacturing cost per unit from $2,200 last year to $2,500 this year; we have to show some progress on our efficiency. You know they (with reverence) authorized our modernization program and in it we promised dramatic reductions in cost per unit."

Manufacturing Manager (Bill Schwartz)

"Sarah, I will give you our best estimate as a function of

volume and taking into consideration all of the cost reduction efforts we can imagine."

	Product Cost/Unit	Total Cost
3,500 units	$2,000	$7,000,000
3,000 units	$2,200	$6,600,000
2,500 units	$2,400	$6,000,000

Note: Bill's previous estimate for 2,500 units was $2,500 per unit—so he is negotiating with Sarah. Last year he produced 3,000 units at $2,200 each, so he is planning on some cost efficiencies to counteract the 6 percent parts and 3 percent labor increases to hold $2,200 each. Sarah is looking for $1,800 per unit. Bill has now said he can do $2,000 to $2,400 per unit depending on sales volume.

We could continue the dialog, but you get the point. You all have been involved in this type of a conversation many times. Frequently it ends up with a forecast being submitted for 2,500 units to be produced at $2,000 cost per unit—total manufacturing cost of $5,000,000 (that's a nice round number). Then, of course, the forecast will be detailed to the second decimal place for each of the components of a complete unit by many people in the organization.

Where has the forecasting process gone wrong? Is Sarah wrong in asking Bill to try to be more cost effective? No, that's her job. Is Bill wrong in explaining to Sarah what influences his cost per unit? No, that's his job.

The problem comes about during the next year when corporate management has one expectation—$2,000 per unit must be well within the organization's potential. Perhaps they will even beat it. Sarah's expectation is something like, "I know it's a stretch for Bill's organization to meet $2,000 per unit, but they will work harder and smarter with a stretch forecast like we submitted." Bill's feelings are something like, "Sarah made that forecast, not me. Every month during the year when we are over the $2,000 per unit forecast I am just going to tell her $2,000 per unit was never possible at 2,500 units and she knew it."

Corporate management is saying they believe there is a 90 percent chance of making $2,000 per unit, Sarah is saying a 50 percent chance, and Bill is saying a 10 percent chance. Therein lies the forecasting dilemma. It is critical that all levels of management agree to what probability of achieving a forecast they are talking about. If Bill's organization actually makes $2,000 per unit with 2,500 units produced, he will consider his organization to have done a fantastic job. Sarah would consider it a good job and corporate management would say if was fair because they were hoping for under $2,000 per unit. By not adequately communicating probabilities of achieving a forecast, the different members of management are operating with different yardsticks for measuring performance.

Of course, the real situations we all face are far more complicated. Sales go up, then down, then up again. Forecasts on new product sales and manufacturing costs are much harder to make then on established products. Some cost reduction programs do not succeed. Vendors have quality problems, assembly problems on the production line cause client backorders, and so on. But the simple conclusions we can reach on forecasting are:

- Forecasts are needed for planning.
- Overly detailed forecasts can be a waste of time to prepare and audit against.
- Communications throughout the organization on the probability of meeting a forecast are critical.

If you would be loved, love and be lovable.
Benjamin Franklin

*A normally useful management tool like a budget can cause some prob-
lems. In your organization, has the Chief Empowerment Officer urged the
unleashing of business creativity?*

24

Budgets

"I have some great news," said Fred Smiley. "The top
salesperson at our largest competitor called me today to ask if
we would be willing to talk to him about hiring on with us.
It's a great stroke of good luck. He sells three times what our
average salesperson does and he has a sterling reputation in
the industry. What do you think?" Joe Chameleon paused
and then said, "Sounds interesting, but there is no way that I
can get our budget for salaries changed to add him. Tell him
to contact us again in six months when we can possibly budget for it."

Are your budgets sometimes too restrictive? Should managers have some way to get exceptions made to the budget
without feeling guilty or feeling like a troublemaker?

"Our production schedule is much lower than we budgeted for since sales just haven't been coming in as forecast," said
Buster Plant. "Do you think we should cut back on our
expenses and lay off some staff? I know our budget has been
approved for the full year, but we may not need as much for
the last four months as we anticipated when we budgeted last
year." Greg Shell responded, "I understand your point,

Buster, but if we don't use this year's budget, we'll have a tough time justifying an increase in budget for next year. You know how budgets generally are made. Management looks at the previous year's expenses and doesn't want to increase too much for next year. You can be a small hero this year by cutting back expenses, but your budget is sure to shrink for next year. What I suggest is that you spend 99 percent of the budget, make sure you take care of this year's needs, and buy things with this year's budget that you are sure to use in the first six months next year. We all will look good by having kept under budget for this year. And we should be able to do very well next year with a good budget and some prepaid expenses."

Do managers play games like this in your organization? Is it ethical? Is it good business? Is it what you encourage?

When budgets are developed, everyone attempts to utilize the best available information. However, business situations frequently change from the November budget time to the next July. A flexible company recognizes that likelihood and is creative in problem solving.

Buster Plant said sales were slow and his production operation didn't need all of the budget it had authorized. Fred Smiley has an opportunity to possibly add a new salesperson from a competitor. The total business might be better off if some of Buster's budget was transferred in the middle of the year to Fred, but, under most bureaucratic, departmental, pyramid paradigm organizations, the situations would probably evolve approximately as Joe Chameleon and Greg Shell concluded. That's a shame!! And it's a signal to a Chief

Empowerment Officer that the budget system is restricting creative business management and limiting the organization to sub-par performance.

"We are delayed in our new product introduction by six months. The development problems were just a lot more complicated than we anticipated," said Frank Cloud. George Rifle, the Director of Sales commented, "Frank, I'm really disappointed to hear that. We've got four people put aside to launch this new product. They are trained and have the marketing and sales effort ready to go when the product is ready. Is there any way that two of them could work with your technical staff to bring the product to commercialization sooner?" "That's a very good idea," said Frank excitedly. "When we build prototypes, we need them tested. If your sales and marketing staff could help us in the internal testing, and then convince a few clients to test our early prototypes, that would be a great help."

Budgets are generally useful but can be misused. Creative problem solving is the most valuable aspect of a business. Frank and George have focused on the business problem first; later they can discuss juggling budgets.

A normally useful management tool like a budget can cause some problems. In your organization, has the Chief Empowerment Officer urged the unleashing of business creativity? The power is within our associates, but we need to unleash it by creating the right atmosphere.

The applause of a single human being is of great consequence.
Samuel Johnson

It has been said that the people in an organization do what management inspects rather than what management expects. Sometimes management has expectations that are not clearly communicated and reinforced in a large organization.

25

Yardsticks of Effectiveness

Is everyone in your organization working toward the same goal with clear yardsticks of effectiveness?

Joann Buck is an accountant who impresses everyone in her organization with how she can handle all the overhead accounts and their allocations. To many people overhead and allocations are strange words, but Joann can explain it to them nicely. "We sell three products. When we sell them and invoice the client it is easy to add up the dollars we received for each product." "Fine so far," her audience would say. "That income for each product we call net sales revenue. The word net is added because it means sales revenue net after all appropriate discounts and returns. The net sales revenue is what we report to the government for our income tax purposes." "So far it sounds easy. When do we get to the hard part?" "Not quite yet," said Joann. "Let's go to the next step. We have many costs that we can directly connect with a given product. For example, all the raw materials used to make Product A are costs that we can definitely associate with Product A. All of the direct labor costs of producing Product A, we can charge as a cost to Product A." "Sure," said her audience, "so you subtract the direct costs from the net sales revenue of Product A and you have the profit, right?" "Wait a minute," Joann would say, "we don't want to go too rapidly. We haven't yet taken overhead and allocations into consideration. You see the engineers at the plant work on all three products, the supervisors work on all three products and the quality control organization checks all three products. Then, our research people work on improvements on all three products and spend money working on a new product not yet available for sale. Our sales people sell all three products, and our legal people work on contracts concerning all three products." "Okay," said the audience, "it sounds like it's not just profit left after you have paid for the costs directly associated with Product A. Somehow Product A needs to pay its fair share of those costs, which you might call overhead." "Now you are getting on to the system," said Joann, "and I happen to be an expert at dividing all of those costs among the various products. You see, management wants every cost to be associated with some product, and we can do it by splitting all the overhead costs with a system of allocations. Some costs we split by product based upon their unit volume. The product with the most units gets charged with the largest percent of the overhead cost. Other costs are charged to each product based on how much labor they take to produce, on net sales revenue for each product, and on the capital investment required to make each product, and so on" "Now I see why this is a complicated subject," the audience comments. "Why split all those overhead cost accounts by product? You are only guessing. You call it allocating."

Joann groans, "I really don't like to do it, because I know how many weak assumptions I am making. But management wants all costs reduced to the three product lines. The trouble is the final profit for Product A versus B versus C depends tremendously on how much of the overhead costs I have allocated to each product line. I'm not happy with the system. Management really should not be asking me to allocate all the overhead costs. There are better ways to measure the effectiveness of the various parts of the organization."

Let's interrupt Joann at this point. Does her conversation sound familiar? In your business, does the allocation of overhead costs take a lot of someone's time? Are the best business decisions made because these allocations are made or in spite of their imprecision? Some businesses operate with a concept of gross margin—net sales income minus costs which are clearly associated with a given product. Someone is given responsibility for maximizing Product A's gross margin. Someone else is given the responsibility for controlling R & D costs, sales costs, etc. The pricing of Product A is based on an analysis of how to maximize gross margin (sometimes called product contribution toward earnings).

This all might seem like accounting details, but it turns out to be important, as we all have experienced, to be sure everyone in the organization is focused on clear performance measuring yardsticks.

Consider the effectiveness yardstick for a manufacturing plant when six new products are needed in a given year. Should the plant be rated on its cost per unit produced or its ability to successfully commercialize six new products that will lead to higher per unit manufacturing cost this year? If the overall business need is for those new products, unit-manufacturing cost must take a secondary priority. That is easier said than done. It takes significant management effort to convince all the people in a plant to put unit cost second in priority to the new products. That is against their traditional emphasis on unit cost reduction.

To achieve emphasis on the six new products for the year, every level of management needs to communicate the goal of new products as first priority, unit cost secondary. Any slips in the communications process and the natural leaning will put the first priority back on unit cost, and potentially harm the introduction of the vital six new products.

In the sales area, is your organization focused on sales units or sales dollars? When a sales force has units as a measure of its performance effectiveness, it will naturally urge lower and lower prices. When sales dollars are the measure of effectiveness yardstick, the sales force will give a somewhat more balanced view considering the price-volume relationship in the marketplace and sometimes urge firm or increased prices to achieve higher sales dollars. Change the effectiveness yardstick and, once a sales force is convinced that you will continue to use that yardstick, the dialog will change to match the new criteria.

Aren't we all the same when it comes to performance yardsticks? We want a reasonable yardstick, one that can be quantified at least somewhat, and we want the yardstick to be broadly understood. The selection of appropriate performance yardsticks is important management work. Have you left a lot of that work to your accountants such as Joann Buck? Or have you taken an active management role in defining and implementing effectiveness yardsticks that suit your business, your business objectives, and your associates?

Controlling the Right Variable

It has been said that the people in an organization do what management *inspects* rather than what management *expects*. The difference between *inspects* and *expects* can be very wide sometimes. The reason people pay attention to what is inspected is because they understand it; the communication is clear and frequently reinforced. Sometimes management has expectations that are not clearly communicated and reinforced in a large organization.

Take the example of managing salaries and wages and consider the grid below:

	Number of People	$ Amount/ Person	Total $ Amount
Exempt	(A)		
Non-exempt			
Wage			
Outside Contractors			
Total			(B)

The area designated by (A) is a headcount control system of exempt personnel. The management concept is, "if this number is managed, then total salary and wages will be under good control." But, in the implementation, if the exempt headcount is the number that is inspected, often there will be some significant changes in non-exempt, wage and outside contractor ranks with not as much reduction in overall salary and wages as were planned by management. A focus on (B), inspected often, will improve the results in (B) where management wants it. A focus on (A) is sub-optimizing, if the real goal is (B).

People in an organization focus on what management inspects as a yardstick of effectiveness.

Happiness doesn't come as a result of getting something we don't have, but rather of recognizing and appreciating what we do have.

Frederick Koenig

*A measure of an effective manager is his or her tolerance for surprises
and ambiguity. Nothing is perfect in the world of communications.*

26

Surprises

Delegation is critical to the development of a management team. When a management hierarchy expects no surprises, they may be stifling their organization's creativity. They may be primarily seeking predictability.

Big Bob Miller had a theme, "I want no surprises. I want to know what controversial issues might come up prior to every meeting. What really gripes me is when my boss or one of my peers tells me about something concerning my organization that I should have heard first from my organization. I don't like to be embarrassed like that." Sound familiar? Do you share some of Big Bob's views? Do you have a Big Bob in your organization?

At first it might appear that Big Bob had a good point. All managers like to have a feeling of being well informed. We all like to project to our boss and our peers that we have the situation under good control. But what price do we pay? By not delegating tasks and communication, we limit our associates to having all subjects reviewed by us. What happens when we are on vacation or traveling? If our organization has to wait until we get back, what opportunities are we missing?

Big Bob didn't care about all that. He took things very personally. "Look," he would say, "I've been burned before with messages going around me. I feel more comfortable knowing exactly what is going on. I feel more comfortable communicating good or bad news myself. I believe in the line organization system. Communications should go up to the top of the line quickly. When a message comes from another organization, which I should have heard from my own organization, it really bugs me. I delegate responsibility to my associates, but I do not feel I can let my staff speak on politically sensitive subjects; that's where I draw the line."

Would you guess that Big Bob was insecure? He certainly was! He was so afraid of something going wrong that he might be criticized for that he missed the opportunity to praise his organization for everything that was going right. Big Bob may be like someone in your organization. He was so self-centered and so insecure that he wouldn't delegate and he insisted on no surprises. Big Bob had hundreds of things go right in his organization, but no one can remember hearing any praises. Everyone can remember the tirades about something going wrong and him hearing about it and being surprised. Big Bob stifled his organization's creativity. Why? Because he wanted no surprises, complete control.

A measure of an effective manager is his or her tolerance for surprises and ambiguity. Nothing is perfect in the world of communications.

When a negative surprise occurs, a creative manager who is a good delegator knows how to handle the situation. First, he listens. Next, he cautions himself not to punish the messenger of bad news. (After all, the messenger isn't necessarily to blame, and people will stop bringing messages if they are chastised for reporting bad news.) Then, he avoids being defensive and gives himself some time to learn more. Generally, after learning more, he finds his organization has used reasonable judgment on the problem area.

The creative delegator also has many occasions when positive surprises occur. He may have delegated a subject to an individual two months ago and now hears about many positive steps toward an improved business. He did not know every step along the way, but he is pleased with the creative solutions. He is making use of all of his people's brains, energy and imaginations. He is not stifling them to channel everything through him. He is not the bottleneck in the creative solution of business problems and the creation of business opportunities.

Are we being too hard on Big Bob? Isn't it fairly natural for a hierarchical organization to operate the way Big Bob would like it to operate? Isn't it too much of a dream to expect management to accept occasional surprises?

In the next ten years, we will see the need for more and more flexible management styles. People want more room to operate, influence their environments and control their own work. Top management may not be comfortable in today's culture. They may want no surprises. But today's culture requires some surprises and a great deal of management flexibility in order to create an atmosphere that unleashes business creativity among all associates and empowers the clients.

If you have some Big Bobs in your organization, you probably should move them to less sensitive jobs. They could be stifling dozens or hundreds of people. You probably will be more successful in your business if you have fewer Big Bobs. They are easy to find once you decide to be sensitive to your corporate culture.

The great thing about getting older is that you don't lose all the other ages you've been.
Madeline L'Engle

My job became my total life. My wife complained that I did not spend any time with the children. I guess I was a workaholic.

27

Managing, Health and Family

A manager is in need of more than a career. The needs for a healthy body and loving relationships outside the corporation are critical to the manager's effectiveness over the long term inside the corporation.

As experienced managers, you know how much a person's performance on the job can suffer from an alcohol or drug problem, a divorce, or other health or personal problems. A manager cannot always help solve such problems, but she certainly cannot afford to ignore them.

Bruce Finkel had a serious set of personal problems which ended in his company going bankrupt, his wife divorcing him and his children being emotionally and physically separated from the potential joys of a loving relationship with their father—financial problems, family problems and emotional problems. Bruce, at age forty, was disappointed with his life. He talked about suicide. Sad, but true. If you were Bruce's manager, how would you have handled the situation? After all, do you have to be responsible for the personal life of your associates as well as their business actions? Do you have to be your brother's keeper?

Bruce later described his situation like this: "Everything just seemed to snowball. Actually, my family life started to go first. Then I let my subordinates at work run the business as they thought it best and, in hindsight, I now see they were making many poor decisions. Oh, they got my okay on major issues, but I didn't take the time to ask many questions. My single pet answer to a three-minute single proposal on a major decision was—'go ahead; sounds good to me.' I was not concentrating. Even if I were concentrating, I probably would have made some poor judgments along with some good ones. But I just copped out on doing my full management job. That's why we went bankrupt. The problems at home led to problems at work, which led to more problems at home. I felt like a failure."

Not all health or family problems are quite so dramatic. But what help could you give to Bruce if you were his manager? Certainly a business does not go bankrupt overnight. Where were the signals of problems? What were the cash flow trends? Was expansion overzealous? Which portion of the business became unprofitable first? Were you monitoring the parts as well as the whole business? Strictly from the business standpoint, what indicators could you have had of a business problem way before it got so serious? When you found some business problems that Bruce could not explain, did you ever ask him if there was any factor outside of work that he felt might be having an effect on the business? After that question, the best thing to do is keep silent and glue your eyes on Bruce's eyes and body language. The longer you keep silent, the more likely you are to get a true response, either directly in words or indirectly in body language, which gives you a tip to probe further.

Should we be our brother's keeper? As managers, it is our job to manage the business, and that means knowing our managers' portion of the business, having indicators established to flag business problems, and to know how to probe and coach when needed.

Joe Trotter told his story. "My job became my total life. My wife complained that I did not spend any time with the children. I told her that my job required me to be away from home so much, especially if I expected to be promoted. She said the job was not worth that much time if we couldn't enjoy life as husband, wife and family. We did enjoy life during our three weeks of vacation. But the other forty-nine weeks were a steady diet of work, work, work. I guess I was a workaholic. But my boss had no gripe, because I was really producing for the company."

Do you know any Joe Trotters? Should a manager worry about Joe? After all, he is really producing a lot of results. Is Joe's manager taking an unfair advantage of Joe's dedication?

If, as a result of Joe's behavior, he ends up with a separation or divorce or alcohol problem, that could lead to him becoming a problem like Bruce. Perhaps now is the time to keep a potential problem from developing. Suggest various alternatives to your Joe, reward and encourage him in small ways for giving somewhat more balance to his efforts. He might even become more efficient and achieve just as much with fewer hours on the job. That happens sometimes.

Another dimension of Joe's behavior is the message it

sends to other associates. If it is perceived that you are encouraging Joe to overdo his work and ignore his family, it could lead to problems with other associates. As the manager, your action or inaction is critical. You are on display all the time. Your associates make judgments based on what they think you are thinking. It is important to work with your Joe for his good and your whole organization's good. No big fanfare is needed, just thoughtful coaching.

Our managers are total people. Their health and family are important as well as their work.

Marianne Feller was a manager whose social life was excellent, in her judgment, and she was very happy with her job in Fort Worth. Then a job opportunity developed for her in Miami. Surely she would be delighted. Wrong! She was crushed. She now had to decide between social life and job opportunity. Men, women, and couples face these problems more and more now that so many couples are both working. As managers, we all know how important it is to help our associates balance their lives.

We can not and should not just tell them what is best for them. But we need to be sympathetic to their personal needs as well as the needs of the business. When personal needs and business needs are balanced, our managers are most productive over the long run. It is career planning. The manager has an important role as a coach. When did you last remind yourself to be a good coach to your associates on balancing the priorities of their personal and business life?

The capacity for hope provides human beings with a sense of destination and the energy to get started.

Norman Cousins

CREATIVE STRATEGIES & TACTICS

Both sales and marketing are critical, but considering them as essentially the same can lead to many poor business judgments.

28

Marketing

Make a better mousetrap, don't tell anyone about it, and wonder why clients have not been beating a path to your door.

In many unsuccessful companies, sales and marketing are considered to be interchangeable words. After all, we call our sales representatives "marketing representatives." Why do we find that happening so often? Is it because sales is considered a less important job and therefore the title "marketing representative" is more attractive and satisfying to the ego of the representative?

In most successful companies, you would be laughed at if you suggested sales and marketing were essentially the same thing. These people feel that marketing is worlds different than sales. P. G. Tracy distinguished quite strongly between sales and marketing, "Marketing is an analysis and planning function that concerns itself with understanding competition, the market forces, the various product offerings, the various prices, the various market segments, the client's needs and wants, the client's current perceptions, and so on. When a marketing strategy is developed, it includes product, service, positioning approach, advertising, pricing, promotion and specific roles for the sales force. The sales force, after extensive input into the marketing plan, is responsible for carrying out the plan with respect to the direct contact with clients. (Of course, sometimes client and prospect contacts are made by mail and/or by phone or distributor to supplement the personal contact of the salesperson.)"

"Marketing oriented business strategies," P. G. continued, "focus on the marketplace for signals to lead the new product or service development, the positioning strategies by segment, the pricing/penetration strategy and the sales approach (direct, by mail, by phone, by distributor, and various combinations)."

"Top management should look to marketing management for leading the way on defining the approach in the marketplace to enhance the businesses' competitive position."

P. G. continued, "One of my favorite marketing examples is the African shoe business. One organization sent its associate to Africa to sell shoes and he came back with the conclusion 'nobody wears shoes; there is no market.' Another company's associate concluded, 'nobody wears shoes; there's a tremendous market opportunity for shoes.' If a product or service is a means of meeting a client need, the key shoe business question in Africa was, 'Is there a need now or can a need be developed in the minds of the clients?'."

P. G. Tracy continued his commentary about the marketing of shoes: "Do you think sandals are a form of shoes? Sure they are; they help a person's foot to be protected from the temperature or hardness of the area to be walked upon.

But our company makes regular shoes and not sandals. That may be too narrow a product offering. We need to consider ourselves as being in the foot-covering business. To meet that need we may have to sell regular shoes for some markets, sandals for some markets, boots for some markets, athletic shoes (even socks), and so on."

It is obvious that you should know the market needs extremely well before you decide to introduce a product or service for that market. Or is it? Haven't we all experienced our companies having a product looking for a market? Haven't we all experienced the disappointment of management when we had to report that their pet product was not well suited for a given market?

Some managers are willing to study the market and the clients extensively before they design a product or service to meet the needs. This is part of the client empowerment concept. Others start from a technology or a product and study the market by trying to sell their product. Dan Robertson described this situation in his words, "I call it disciplined marketing and disciplined business management. I encourage a great deal of market research/understanding of client's needs, competitive trends, growth of markets, and so on.) and marketing research (testing different products, price and promotion combinations). It takes a great deal of discipline to follow the results of the studies. Time and time again we have been tempted to commercialize or broadly distribute a product that did poorly in its test markets. There are so many corporate pressures to increase production and hope that the product will be better received than in the early tests.

Discipline is necessary to believe the test markets, fix the problem and then carefully go through the test market phase again. It sounds easy but when competition is getting the sales, it is tempting to launch what you know to be a product that isn't right for the market needs. Discipline is difficult but very important."

"Then," Dan continued, "when the product is on target, well-planned sales and communications strategies are critical. It is a marketing question to decide whether the offering should be made through a distributor, by our own sales force, by phone, over the Internet, and so on. The timing of a sales campaign is a marketing decision. The content and timing of the advertising and promotion program is also a marketing responsibility."

Salespeople know a great deal about today's clients, today's products and today's competitive offerings. Salespeople are excellent at providing input, but, as P. G. Tracy pointed out, it is very important to also have input to your marketing decisions from independent studies. The important marketing and business decisions cannot be left to salespeople alone. They do not have enough information to make the tough business decisions.

Is your business a strong advocate of disciplined marketing? Have you ever done marketing research and praised it when it supported your prior hypothesis, but ignored it if it didn't? Is your sole input on the market and your offering versus the competitors from your salespeople? Can you honestly say you have a Dan Robertson or a P. G. Tracy in your company? Do you listen to them?

The role of marketing is often misunderstood and yet its effective management is critical to the success of any business. Marketing, when done with the appropriate discipline, is very important to the profitability of a business.

Do you have specific market needs for your research and development people to aim for? Dan Robertson did. His market research people would define the market niche that was desired, the product specifications that would provide a leadership position in the niche and a maximum product cost to meet the market pricing needs of the future and still have a reasonable profit. Dan Robertson's R & D people sometimes were upset at the tightness of the product specifications and the low product cost that was set as a maximum. Dan had an excellent track record, so they set their creative energies toward meeting the needs. Sure, there was frequent negotiation between the marketing people and the R & D people on the product specifications and cost, but the marketplace was the judge. When a prototype was developed, it was field-tested. Dan insisted on very early evaluation of prototypes. That was part of his disciplined marketing approach. How do you guide your company's R & D?

Dan Robertson learned one excellent lesson from P. G. Tracy—how to learn from competitors' market research tests. P. G. Tracy explained, "I have found that we can learn about as much from a competitors' test markets as we can from our own and we save all the product development costs. If our competitor is test marketing in a certain part of the country, we buy some of his product and have it analyzed in our lab. Then we survey purchasers of his product to find the client's degree of satisfaction. We can learn a lot for a low cost. It helps us to better understand the market for our own products or service test markets."

Dan and P. G. would suggest that marketing is a profession with a substantial difference in required expertise than sales. Both sales and marketing are critical, but considering them as essentially the same can lead to many poor business judgments.

Someone is truly human and becomes his true self by overlooking himself and focusing outward.

Victor Frankl

We have had a personnel system that de-motivates half the sales force every year. We rate everyone versus each other so half find they are below average. I'll never get 100 percent professionals that way.

29

Selling

Sales is a noble profession. Salespeople are the unique contributors who link the business to its clients. Wow, is that link critical!

Why is it when surveys are taken, ranking professions with high prestige that sales positions do not rate very high? Is it because the general public's opinion of a salesperson is one of a semi-pro rather than a pro? Is selling a profession that many people feel requires less intellectual ability than other professions?

No matter how you answered those three questions, as a practicing manager you know how critical the link is between your company and your clients. Salespeople uniquely provide that link.

Walter Simmons was the top salesperson in his company for years. Walter's feelings were, "I'm a professional piano salesman. I love music. I love pianos, and I love to share my pleasure with others. It is important to me that my clients are happy with their piano and their buying experience. I live in this community and work here. My friends are also my clients. When one client is happy, I get several other referrals from him to help me sell several others." People asked Walter what his secret was and he would say, "I love what I do. It seems that clients really enjoy the fact that I sit at the piano and play jazz or classical music or anything to demonstrate the piano to them. But what really turns them on is when I almost disassemble the piano in front of them and show them how fine the inside construction is. Most piano salesmen cannot play Chopin or Rachmaninoff, and hardly any salesman can both play and describe the internal construction of a piano as I can. I work at keeping up on the technical details."

If there were four piano outlets in Walter's city, which one would you think would sell the most pianos? Sure, Walter's store would be a leader, probably No. 1. Does that mean he is selling the most popular brand of piano? Not at all! Walter needs a place to work, one of the top five brands of pianos and a lot of personal freedom to sell, using his time-proven techniques. Walter takes a lot of time with each client and each client knows they have been dealing with a pro. Walter's clients do not complain about price very much. Why? Because Walter has them so convinced of the piano's quality that they believe the price he offers is a fair one. When Walter demonstrates a lower priced piano he does not talk it down; he describes all its features, demonstrates its tone and promotes it as the best value on the market in that lower price range. Of course, he demonstrates higher priced models also, describing the extra features they offer. Walter is a pro. Then how come he can take even the fifth most popular piano brand in the country and make it No. 1 in his city? Because he is a sales pro and pros make a big difference.

Would you like to have one hundred Walters in your sales organization? How many do you have now? Why is it that you feel less than 20 percent of your sales force could come close to being Walters?

Susie Jasper told Walter, "My sales organization has thirty-six sales people and I would only put three or maybe four in your class. We have three or four real pros. But that is not enough to meet the sales targets we want to reach. Oh, how I would love to have eighteen pros out of thirty-six." Walter responded in this way to Susie. "First, why not thirty-six out of thirty-six? Second, tell me about the sales managers who these thirty-six salespeople report to. Third, tell me more about Susie's philosophy of management." "Wow," said Susie, "you sound like you are well prepared on this subject." "Sure," said Walter, "I'm a professional salesperson and my experience has taught me how to dig beneath the surface."

The dialogue went on and on until Susie finally summarized, "Walter, you have done me a valuable service. Here is how I now see the situation. There are forty people involved in my business, my three sales managers, my 36 salespeople, and myself. Forty people's personal egos, personal paychecks and personal careers need to be considered. Each of the forty has something valuable to contribute to the growth of the others and the growth of our business. So you jogged my thinking in an important way."

"Next," continued Susie, "I have concluded that my group is just as bright and just as dedicated as any of my competitors' sales organizations; I don't have a bunch of duds—maybe one or two might do better elsewhere, but over 90 percent of my people have the potential to be pros." Walter interrupted, "I like that phrase, 'potential to be pros' but I would suggest that 100 percent probably have the potential. You may just elect to focus on 90 percent, that's a good start." "Right again," said Susie. "As I reflect on the past year, we have focused on getting better results but have done very little training. Like you, Walter, my sales managers and my salespeople could greatly benefit by having more detailed product knowledge. I can help them in several ways on that. Also, exchanging unique selling approaches with each other could be helpful. In this market there are about five hundred salespeople. My goal would be to have my thirty-six salespeople, if you could ever rank them, all among the top one hundred of the five hundred in the market. Wow, that would give us a dynamite sales team. Why, our sales would be twice what they are today. Why, we would move from No. 3 to No. 2 in the market." "Sounds like you are getting really enthusiastic about the prospects for growth," said Walter, "that's important. Set your goals with enthusiasm but be sure to get your people involved individually as well as a group." "Sure," said Susie, "and I plan to focus on a great deal of positive reinforcement. Coaching by the managers will be key, and I personally have a lot of work to do to create the right atmosphere for each individual in the organization. You know, we have had a personnel system which de-motivates half the sales force every year. We rate everyone versus each other so half find they are below average. I'll never get 100 percent professionals that way. I need to work on ways to have each person outdo himself and not worry about his position versus all the others. That won't be easy, but I think I can do it because they all have different territories. Each territory and each individual is different. Some things we all need to know and to do exactly the same. Other things can be variable by territory. This is going to be an exciting year. Thanks, Walter."

Can you thank Walter? Do you have a problem or opportunity like Susie's? Selling and salespeople—oh, so important to a business.

Joe Lisper decided to try sales and was involved in an extensive sales training program for two months. His product was a toothbrush. His manager was very concerned about his ability to succeed in sales because of his very pronounced lisp.

The first week of actual selling was over and the salespeople were all assembled. Sure enough, out of 12 salespeople, Joe was number 12 and not even close to number 11. His manager suggested he review all his training notes and try harder the next week. The next week—still number 12 out of 12.

The manager then suggested to Joe that he talk to the top three salespeople and get some tips from them. Sure enough, the next week Joe was number 1 out of 12. Every salesperson and the manager couldn't believe the numbers. How had Joe done it? "Well," lisped Joe, "it was this way. I got a real good tip from one of the top salespeople. He told me I needed a gimmick. Without a gimmick I'd never sell many toothbrushes, but with one I could sell thousands. He told me every salesperson had to develop his own gimmick." "So what was your gimmick?" chimed the salespeople in a chorus. "Well, I set up my entire toothbrush supply in Grand Central Station in New York. I knew I needed a lot of people to sell a lot of toothbrushes. Then, I put a card table next to me with a big bowl of potato chips and a special dip. As people came by, I'd offer them a potato chip and dip. Most of them would try the dip and say, 'That's good. What's the recipe?' Then I would say 'Sour cream and horse manure.' They'd try to spit up what they'd just swallowed. Then I'd say, 'Want to buy a toothbrush?'"

Although this old Joe Lisper story was designed for a chuckle, professional selling involves a lot more than a gimmick. Walter Simmons provided the sound advice—professionalism, training, hard work and enthusiasm. A company's successful salespeople deserve major recognition for their tremendous contribution to the short and long-term health of the business.

It is only with the heart that one can see rightly.
What is essential is invisible to the eye.
Antoine de Saint-Exupery

The two-call sale might occur on two different days or have one "call" the first five minutes and the second "call" the next five minutes.

30

The Two-Call Sale

The psychology of buying and selling is well documented. The close has been described in many ways as the most critical element in a sales call. The two-call sale is a concept that does not contradict all the guidance we have heard in the past, but it carries the sales-call strategy to a further refined plane of expertise.

Situation No. 1

Our financial investment program is just for you. It's a perfect tax shelter, and so on.

(Assumption—I know all your needs and the product I have to offer is just perfect for you. Arrogant, pushy, presumptuous.)

Situation No. 2

Everyone has different financial needs. We have developed a computer program that takes your current financial situation, your financial objectives, your family situation, your business situation, and so on, all into consideration before we recommend a specific financial service.

(Assumption—The prospect is willing to take a lot of

time to complete a lengthy questionnaire on detailed financial status that is very personal and confidential, to a person he has only recently met. Uncomfortable, strained, risky.)

Situation number 1 is focusing on the close before adequate probing and questioning has been done to identify the true needs of the prospect. Not a good technique, but one we see every day in sales situations. Sales people have been trained to close. Get the sale. If the prospect shows even a little interest, ask for the order. In small ticket items it can work fine. "Would you like the yellow Penn tennis balls for $2.59 a can or the white Wilson balls for $2.19 a can?" Even then, the client might ask, "What does this mean; one is recommended for hard surfaces and one for soft surfaces?" Now the client's need to play on soft surfaces has influenced the purchasing decision and the salesperson needs to be aware of the need to probe a bit, even on small ticket items. But a big-ticket item certainly needs considerable questioning and probing to be sure the salesperson is recommending the right product or service to achieve the result the client is seeking. "Oh, I didn't realize you were going to have a family of five try to fit into this two-door compact car I was showing you."

Situation number 2 is a form of very extensive probing and questioning but in a very impersonal way. Most people recoil from this type of a sales appeal because it is so impersonal and psychologically uncomfortable. "I'm an individual with needs, desires, wants, opinions, habits, and so on, and I prefer to have a professional salesperson talk to me on my terms rather than make me fit into his or her predetermined mold for a computer analysis."

The two-call sale might occur on two different days or have one "call" the first five minutes and the second "call" the next five minutes. In big purchases, the length of the first call is necessarily quite long. The client is offended if the second call has been started well before the first call is completed.

The first call is the needs clarification, questioning, probing, and so on. Effective probing in a polite, friendly manner is a salesperson's most powerful sales tool! Ask a question, then keep quiet and listen intently to the prospect's comments. Probe further for other needs. Summarize for clarification. All of this phase is the first call. Do not cut it short! Ask the client if there are any other thoughts he feels you should know about. Ask some test questions, "Are X, Y or Z important to you?" "How about A or B?"

Between the first and second sales call is the most creative challenge for the outstanding sales person. How am I going to mesh all of this prospect's needs and desires with the offerings of products and services my company has for sale? Is there a fit at all? Can I meet at least most of the prospect's needs? How should I present the offering to the prospect—verbally, as a written proposal, now, next week, by myself, with my boss? This is crunch time for a salesperson in a very short time—perhaps a few seconds or at most a minute—the salesperson needs to decide how to proceed to the second call. This is an absolutely critical part of any sales transaction.

The second call can take many forms but is the place where the offering is made, trial closes occur, responding to objections and, of course, the final close are included. All of these steps are critical, but the second call is only as effective as the first call and the period between the first and second call permit it to be. Great second calls depend on great first calls and the creativity between calls. The offering to the prospect should be in his language. "As I understand it, you were looking for this, that and the other thing. My company has an excellent solution to this and that and quite a good solution to the other thing." If your product or service has ten benefits and three are critical to this prospect, focus on those three in your offering; don't belabor all ten. Speak to the needs and specifics as described by the prospect in his language. Don't force the prospect to listen to your vocabulary or jargon. It means putting yourself into the prospect's "state of mind."

Fred Smiley always uses a two-call sales approach; he's a professional. But many less experienced salespeople have heard so much about the close that they skip the first sales call and the creative period between sales calls. Fred Smiley conducts his sales calls like this 100 percent of the time. Think of the effectiveness of your sales force if every salesperson used the two-call sale approach every time!

The greatest discovery of my generation is that human beings can alter their lives by altering their attitudes of mind.
William James

One of the most critical variables in pricing is determining the client's overall perception of your total offering versus competition.

31

Pricing

If your product or service is not meeting an important need or want in the marketplace, do not expect people to pay a lot for it. There is a price/volume relationship in every market for every offering and it is critical that a successful business person understands the relationship (even if ever so vaguely).

One day a woman visited a butcher shop and asked about the price of the lamb chops. The owner said, "The lamb chops are $5.00 per pound." The woman felt that the price was too high, so she went to a nearby butcher shop. She asked, "How much are your lamb chops?" The butcher said, "$1.50 per pound." "Good," said the woman, "I'll take four pounds." "I'm sorry, we are out of lamb chops today," said the butcher. Thereupon, the woman quickly went to the first butcher to tell him about the $1.50 per pound price. He responded, "When I'm out of lamb chops I charge $1.50 per pound too." Supply, demand and pricing are obviously closely related.

As every manager knows, pricing must be done in the full context of the competitor's price offerings as well as the full non-price offering of your company and your competitors. A client buys a product for a price but also is buying the continued good service from the supplier, terms of payment, delivery schedules, inventory arrangements, packaging of the product, and so on.

A plastic supplier once was very surprised that a particular client was very anxious to receive the tiny plastic pellets in a box of certain dimensions. At first, the supplier thought the client must have some new unloading equipment. Eventually, the supplier found that the box of certain dimensions was used as a shipping container for the parts the client was molding. The carton it was shipped in significantly enhanced the perceived value of the offering of the plastic pellets.

Price lists are developed to try to meet the clients' needs for a product of good value and the supplier's needs to make a profit. However, on many occasions the price list does not exactly meet the needs of every client. Special negotiations by client are then the natural outcome. Many marketing managers wish such headaches would go away but, unfortunately, so might the clients go away. The typical salesperson just tries to do his job of selling and meeting needs account by account. If the price list meets the need or the latest promotional offering meets the need, the salesperson is happy. If the client asks for a lower price than the salesperson is authorized to give, a marketing manager needs to get involved. The salesperson is interested in a special price for this one case. The marketing manager must weigh if the special price is one he wants to apply to all clients in a similar set of circumstances. A quick profit calculation must be made with the high price/low volume situation being compared with a lower price/higher volume potential. Pricing is that way—cut and try, cut and try. Show me the manager who says list price for every client is the way it is always going to be and I will show you a manager who will gradually lose much of his business to competition.

Clients like a bargain. They would rather buy a product for $2.00 that is normally $3.00 than to have you reduce the list price to $2.00. They would have the same product offering at the $2.00 price but they would be missing something— the personal satisfaction of having saved 33 percent. Even the most rational of clients likes to think that they got a bargain. It applies when a person is buying a house, a car, ketchup or an industrial product. The list price is an indication of product value. When no other reliable information is available, clients use list price as a proxy for quality and value. They perceive high-priced items as more valuable than low-priced items. The key is to have a high quality and value image and price the product competitively enough to gain market share.

The first principle of course is product value. If the product does not fit the client's needs, it is of no use to offer it at a discounted price. Once the product or service is found to meet the client's needs, then it is negotiation time.

Generally, a sales force will request the lowest possible prices to help them become competitive in the marketplace. This is especially true if the yardstick for measuring the salesperson's performance is unit sales rather than dollar sales or dollar gross profit, or contribution toward earnings. It is extremely helpful to have sales revenue or gross profit contribution as a sales effectiveness measurement tool.

Understanding the price/volume relationships is one of the most critical tasks in setting prices. Price/volume data are not easy to develop but by controlled pricing experiments it is possible to take much of the guesswork out of the pricing decisions.

There are times for price increases and times for price decreases. One of the most critical variables in pricing is determining the client's overall perception of your total offering versus competition. Perception is the whole question—actual prices are secondary to price perceptions. Price perceptions are reality because they are the basis for the client's buying decisions.

Market research on pricing and the total offering in competition is valuable. Systematic procedures to capture the essence of the client/salesperson pricing conversations are vital to good pricing programs.

Pricing is one of the most critical business decisions that a business organization makes. Are you exploring your pricing decisions in enough depth? Do you have information about the market independent from your salespeople to supplement their requests for lower prices? What is value to your client? What are you doing to empower your client?

**Take a chance!
All life is a chance. The person who goes the furthest
is generally the one who is willing to do and dare.**
Dale Carnegie

Negotiation is a technique or skill that every effective manager does well either instinctively or through years of experience.

32

Negotiations by Any Other Name

There are hundreds of occasions in a business year when a manager is a major participant in a negotiation. Outstanding business managers have learned how to effectively negotiate in a broad variety of situations.

Fred Smiley telephoned the president of a corporation with $100 million sales and said, "I am Fred Smiley from the XYZ Corporation. We haven't met, but I believe I can describe to you an opportunity for our corporations to work together jointly that would be very attractive for both of us." The corporation president asked Fred a few questions and then Fred continued, "We have been studying your company and its place in the market. If you could share two hours with us, I believe it would be well worth your time. I'd like to discuss the situation with you face-to-face. I don't have a formal presentation to make. It would be great if we could meet in some private place where we could have a chart pad or two or a blackboard so we could each jot down our key thoughts. Good, Friday at 10:00 a.m. in your office will be fine." Fred was starting a negotiation by creating a friendly atmosphere but with a certain amount of suspense. He could have told the president what he had to offer during this initial phone call, but if he had, he would have been giving up a better opportunity for a two-hour face-to-face discussion. In many ways, Fred was selling himself to reach the next step of exploring opportunities with the president. Fred was an experienced negotiator with the title of Salesman.

Negotiation goes by many names — selling, buying, persuasion, mediation, conciliation, influencing and managing. Negotiation takes place when two or more people or groups are seeking a mutually acceptable solution to a situation that is important to all parties concerned.

Buster Plant frequently was involved in labor-management negotiations in his factory. His years of experience he describes as follows, "The step that people refer to as contract negotiations is only one step in a long series of negotiation steps which occur before and after the formal contract negotiations. The atmosphere created in the plant on a day-to-day, situation-by-situation basis is the real starting point of negotiations. I need to know my job and my associates. I need to have respect for them and show it in my daily decisions. When there is good mutual respect and open communications, the final negotiation of contract terms can go quite smoothly. If we have done our homework over the past year, we should not be surprised by any union request, and they won't be surprised by our plans for the future of the business. We feel that all effective negotiations are the result of a long process that occurs each day throughout the year where small decisions are reached after appropriate discussion. Our goal is to work with the union representatives so that we can jointly focus on what appears to be in the best interest of both parties. We have found that it is best not to crystallize our position versus their position. We find the best contract solutions are ones where each party describes its basic interests rather than just its position."

"For example, our plant has been producing two major product lines over the past fifteen years. These product lines required certain specific skills of our associates. In the marketplace, we were losing business on one product line because it was based on old technology. The other product line was healthy, but it had little growth. Management decided to put a third product at our plant based on new technology which would gradually replace our weak product line. But the problem was that the new product line required many fewer people to produce it and those people needed specific skills. The union was very concerned about its members but understood, after considerable discussion, that the company and its associates were best served by introducing the new high technology product and phasing out the old one. Fortunately, the new product was going to be made at our plant which was better than losing the old product and having nothing to replace it. The initial interests of the company and the union were, in short:

Company Interests	Union Interests
Phase out one product for another	Provide jobs for the people now employed
Reduce the total number of associates employed	Seek best possible wages for associates
Increase average technical skill level of associates to produce the new product	

By discussing basic interests rather than formal positions, we were able to negotiate a common set of interests that were acceptable to all.

Common Interests/Joint Plan
♦ Establish a timetable for phase-in of the new product.
♦ Give present associates an opportunity to receive special training to see if they can reach the technical skill necessary on the new product.
♦ Promote those who are successful in reaching the technical skill so they receive more income.
♦ Provide some early retirement and out-placement services (including several months' pay) to those who couldn't reach the technical proficiency required.

Buster Plant was an expert in the field of negotiation. Sure, the solution to the dilemma sounds reasonable, but how many experienced managers have seen sparks fly over a situation like this? The union sometimes tries to show management that it is so powerful that it will strike the plant if any associates are dismissed for lack of work. The company sometimes says it can play hard ball too and will just put the new product at another plant in another part of the country. Each takes a position that it feels is necessary to show its strength and independence.

Negotiation based on the interests of the parties is not weakness or compromise. It is merely a sound route for two or more people or groups to seek a mutually acceptable solution to a situation that is important to all parties concerned.

It is win/win negotiation.

Buster Plant had a close friend who was buying a property that he was going to use as a landscaping and garden shop. The owners were asking $380,000 for the property, which was considerably more than Buster's friend wanted to pay, but he felt the land and location were perfect for his needs. Many people would suggest that Buster's friend make an extremely low offer (perhaps $200,000) with full expectation that the owner probably would not accept it but at least they could then consider splitting the difference, after some haggling, and reach $290,000, which was acceptable to Buster's friend. But Buster gave his friend other advice. "Perhaps the owner has some tax considerations or other needs that would make it more desirable for him to receive the money over several years. Before you offer a price, why don't you ask a few questions such as:

- Would you consider several payments over a few years?

- Do you want to continue to own properties? Would you consider swapping this property for another one in another part of town?

- Do you have any suggestions on who would be a reliable person who might be interested in helping me manage the landscaping business?

In other words, explore each other's interests before crystallizing the discussion on the specific price."

Buster's friend thought this was the long, slow way to negotiate but he agreed to try it since he respected Buster's track record in the field of negotiations. Not every negotiation goes this smoothly, but the conclusion was great for all parties. Buster's friend ended up meeting his needs and the owner's needs. He paid $100,000 at closing for the property with five follow-up annual payments of $40,000 each. That is a total of $300,000 but gave the previous owner a better tax situation and Buster's friend a chance to earn some money in the landscaping business to help pay the $40,000 per year payments. Meanwhile, the money he had available ($290,000 he was prepared to pay up front versus the $100,00 he had to pay — a difference of $190,000) could be invested at an attractive interest rate.

The owner did not want to swap properties, but he did suggest a reliable person to help manage the landscaping business. Buster's friend agreed to employ that person, the owner's nephew, for six months on a trial basis.

Sales situations are truly negotiation sessions. The professional salesperson spends some time probing for the potential buyer's needs or hot buttons. The product, price, terms, delivery, and so on are all suggested to meet the client's needs. When a salesperson starts out presenting wares without probing extensively, it becomes a sales pitch. A salesperson with a gift of gab is nowhere near as valuable as a salesperson with a gift of probing and listening. That's negotiation — interest clarification and then jointly developing a proposal that is mutually acceptable. Negotiation in sales situations takes time, but time spent up front probing and listening increases the likelihood of a sale tremendously. Oh, how many times we have been offended by a salesperson who told us about his product in depth, before he knew our needs. A poor salesperson is frequently a poor listener and negotiator.

It's budget time and you want to convince management that your group's budget should be 20 percent higher next year. You call your friend, Buster Plant. "Buster, how would you approach this negotiation? Should I describe how important it is that we do more projects next year? Should I shoot for a 50 percent increase and then compromise to 20 percent, which I really feel is right for the business? What would you suggest?" "Well," says Buster, "first of all, I am glad you recognized this as a negotiation situation. Before you ask for 20 percent or 50 percent more, or whatever, I suggest you ask yourself and others some questions."

"What are your management's alternatives for budget monies? What other projects will people be asking top management to budget for? What is the likely payoff of your projects versus those others? What has your track record been in the last few years on results versus budget? Do you need all the money starting the first of the year or can your projects appropriately phase in during the year? Do you have all the people to conduct the projects or is that another issue beside the budget dollars? Have you prepared your management for the possibility of needing more budget? When is the final date when all budgets need to be submitted? What support from other groups would be helpful in your quest for additional budget?"

Buster did it again; he changed a negotiation of positions into an exploration of interests. It takes more time up front, but it makes your proposal more likely to succeed.

Virtually every personnel discussion is a negotiation session. "I would like to be considered for a job in manufacturing supervision," says the associate in search of some career encouragement and guidance. "Frankly," says her boss, "we hadn't planned that for you. We thought you were very happy in your planning assignment and we in management do not feel a manufacturing supervisory job is a good fit." You can see a positional bargaining session starting. Both sides have staked out a position and now it could be tension time, anxiety time. Suppose instead the associate had really explored her own interests:

♦ she wanted to try something new; she was becoming bored with the planning job

♦ she wanted to get back into supervisory work anywhere — sales, finance or manufacturing

♦ she wanted to move to another part of the country

Now that is broader than asking for a manufacturing supervision job directly. When she asked her boss for some career encouragement and guidance with this broader expression of interests, her boss said, "Your thoughts raise several possibilities. We have a need for your talent as a financial group supervisor in Houston or a sales group supervisor in Denver." All three of her interests could be met — something new, something supervisory and something in another part of the country, and she now had two options and an upbeat career conversation rather than a tension-filled discussion about the unavailability of a manufacturing supervision job.

Negotiation is a technique or skill that every effective manager does well either instinctively or through years of experience. As managers, we can all learn a lot from experts such as Buster Plant to strive for win/win negotiations. Negotiation skills are mostly common sense but some people have been in the business world for twenty years and not learned the basic skills of negotiation. Negotiation by any other name is critical in the successful business career of a manager.

A very savvy mother of two and four year old girls tells this story from her child-raising experiences.

"The girls are generally very good, but on this occasion I had to use the Kitchen Timer Negotiation Approach. They were arguing over who should play with a certain toy. I told them that I would put them each in a chair looking at each other and set the kitchen timer for one minute. They were to talk to each other for a minute to solve the problem and at the end of a minute tell me the conclusion. It worked like a charm and I now step back and ask them to use the Kitchen Timer Negotiation Approach whenever the situation needs to have a sharing process."

Adults could learn a lesson from this wise mother's solution. Sometimes all we need is a third-party who loves (or at least respects) the two people who are arguing to figuratively (or literally) set the one-minute kitchen timer and require that we work out our differences.

We are no greater than our dreams. Dreams are the touchstones of our characters.
Henry David Thoreau

Individuals who want to significantly influence their own destiny and who want to unleash their business creativity, need to be given a positive atmosphere which engenders teamwork, open communication and mutual respect.

33

Avoid Bureaucracy Like the Plague

Bureaucracy in business is one of the most negative influences on profitability and one of the most negative influences on unleashing business creativity...to empower your clients. Let's review where bureaucracy comes from and why it persists unless management consciously and publicly strives to avoid it like the plague.

Our society for hundreds and thousands of years has been influenced by the bureaucracy paradigm. We even are inclined to draw pyramids with the "chief" at the top and the "workers" at the bottom. We talk about "job levels" with the same pyramid picture in our minds. The pyramid paradigm is reinforced across all elements of society:

* Generals - captains - sergeants - privates
* Cardinals - bishops - priests - parishioners
* President - manager - supervisor - individual contributor
* Salary - non-exempt salary - wage

Job levels are often given numbers. A level 16 Vice President has a level 14 General Manager reporting to her...on down, in the pyramid image to an entry level clerical worker at level 1. There is an extensive consulting infrastructure of "Personnel" or "Human Resources" experts who help companies determine what "level" a job should be and what its compensation scale should be based on:

1. the dollar responsibility of the person in the position,
2. the number of people managed by the person in the position, and
3. the training, experience and skill level required of the person in the position.

In the interest of "fairness," positions are given a range of job levels say 7 through 9 to permit a person to enter at 7 and progress to 9 over time with experience and positive contributions.

In recent years, we have heard about "de-layering," which results in the President of a corporation only being four levels from an entry-level associate when previously they had been eight levels of supervision removed. The benefits of "de-layering" are:

1. lower costs,
2. more responsibility and authority for people who are close to the problems and solutions of the business,
3. better communications on important business issues,
4. better likelihood of all business members knowing each other personally and working together as a team, and
5. better likelihood of empowering the clients.

Bureaucracy not only comes from tall pyramids but also

from wide pyramids. We've all experienced where it is expected that you receive the approval of your manager before you can approach another manager in a different department to solve a business problem. This has become known as "Turf Battles" where each manager protects his organization from information sources outside of approved channels.

You'd think this would only happen in huge organizations like the government, but I have seen it in full force in a 17-person company. Two people with adjacent offices were not allowed to work together to satisfy a client unless they got approval from each of their managers for every case. The owner of this small company told me, when I uncovered the problem for him, "I've created this organizational system over the past 12 years, and encouraged it, so I am not comfortable emotionally changing it. However, if you buy this business, I wouldn't be surprised to see you operate more efficiently with fewer people." We did buy the business and operated it with fewer people all considered as associates and all talking to each other to resolve client issues daily. Costs were lower, the clients were served and each of the associates felt better about being an important part of the business.

"Turf battles," "job levels" and "pecking orders" are the everyday material for office gossip and office politics. When a tremendous amount of human energy is being spent on bureaucracy-related issues, you can be sure that an organization is not efficiently and effectively satisfying its clients, associates and investors.

Individuals who want to significantly influence their own

destiny and who want to unleash their business creativity, need to be given a positive atmosphere which engenders teamwork, open communication and mutual respect. Rigid organization charts and job descriptions inhibit creativity in business and government.

It is entirely possible to operate a business without an organization chart and job descriptions. Creative human resources approaches are needed. For example, the annual performance review needs to be rethought, restructured and possibly eliminated in its present form.

Consider the scenario where 100 people are being evaluated and the company's rules are that 15 must be rated A, 35 B, 35 C and 15 D. When the reviews are completed, half of the 100 feel they are below average because they got C or D ratings. Emotionally destructive to any organization. It happens very often in organizations with the rationalizations:

1. "Everybody should know where they stand."
2. "Not everyone can be paid at the top of the pay scale."
3. "My hands are tied. I had to give 50 percent C's and D's."

There are many creative and positive ways to get around these negative atmosphere situations. But first, managers need to decide that "unleashing business creativity to empower your clients" is much more important to the success of the business than "administering like we always have."

What is the paradigm in your organization? Is every associate empowered? Is the established bureaucracy part of your business strength or business problem? Does bureaucracy in your organization inhibit the enhancement of your core competency? Are your clients empowered?

You will become as small as your controlling desire; as great as your dominant aspiration.
James Allan

The Year 2000 & Beyond

Work is such a large part of a person's life; working in an empowering environment makes life more satisfying and enjoyable.

34

The Empowering Environment

It isn't possible to motivate another person; motivation comes from within. The manager, however, does have the option of creating an empowering environment so that all associates are comfortable motivating themselves.

This is efficient, effective and humane management. Every individual has the desire to be part of a vibrant community to enhance their self-esteem and to satisfy their ego. Work is such a large part of a person's life; working in an empowering environment makes life more satisfying and enjoyable.

A positive atmosphere in a motivated team of individuals in a business is achievable by emphasizing two basic principles:

♦ Managers must provide the leadership and vision for the corporate mission. Only with effective leadership over many years, can a business sustain its core competency and competitive advantage.

♦ A key value of the leaders needs to be the desire to create an empowering environment that unleashes business creativity to empower the clients.

Corporate cultures are easy to recognize but hard to precisely define. Every company and business has a culture, which happened by plan or by incremental steps over time. Changing a corporate culture is a major project because many associates' attitudes need to adjust. With steady leadership and patience, a large organization may take three to five years to make a major change in its corporate culture. A start-up company can start with the principles it believes in and doesn't have to undergo massive changes in the attitudes of its associates as it grows.

The start in an analysis of a corporate culture is considering the management approach.

Management Approach

Control

Participation

Flexible teams

Control is a common management approach and, over the years, it spawned the concept of "span of control" — how many people can one person effectively supervise? The control approach led to the pyramid paradigm, and the relationship structure of manager/supervisor/employee.

Management Approach	Paradigm	Relationship
Control	Pyramid	Employees
Participation	Democratic pyramid	Employees
Flexible teams	Fluid structure	Associates

Over time, many organizations found that associates wanted participation and a relaxation of some of the rigidities of the pyramid bureaucratic structures and such changes were important for a business to be competitively effective.

The management approach of flexible teams, the paradigm of a fluid structure and the relationship of associates provides the empowering atmosphere to unleash business creativity and empower your clients.

Is everyone comfortable in an atmosphere of flexible teams, a fluid structure and the relationship of associates? No, not initially. Peoples' emotional comfort is directly related to their attitude toward risk and reward in the organizational setting.

Organizational Culture Alternatives

	Reward	
	Avoid Punishment	Positive Recognition
Old Approaches (Low risk)		
Risk		
New Approaches (High Risk)		

On the risk scale, some people are very accustomed to old approaches that entail low risk; others want new approaches and are comfortable with high risk. On the reward scale, many people want positive recognition for their work, while others are content to at least avoid the negative impact of punishment.

Organizational Culture Alternatives

	Reward	
	Avoid Punishment	Positive Recognition
Old Approaches (Low risk)	Bureaucracy (Routine/Procedures)	
Risk		
New Approaches (High Risk)		

Bureaucracy is the common format for organizations that operate in the area of low risk and avoiding punishment as the reward. Jobs have a routine, rigid job descriptions and company procedures.

Organizational Culture Alternatives

	Reward	
	Avoid Punishment	Positive Recognition
Old Approaches (Low risk)		
Risk		
New Approaches (High Risk)		Entrepreneurial (Innovative/Fun)

The entrepreneurial quadrant is innovative, creative and fun, but it involves high risk emotionally. Many people think they would enjoy working in this organization culture as compared to bureaucratic organizations.

Organizational Culture Alternatives

	Reward	
	Avoid Punishment	*Positive Recognition*
Old Approaches		*Efficient*
(Low risk)		*(Please the boss)*
New Approaches		
(High Risk)		

Risk (label on left side)

For those people who want the positive recognition but find themselves in an organization which fosters old approaches, being efficient and pleasing the boss is a reasonable alternative.

Organizational Culture Alternatives

	Reward	
	Avoid Punishment	*Positive Recognition*
Old Approaches		
(Low risk)		
New Approaches	*Russian*	
(High Risk)	*roulette*	

Risk (label on left side)

We've labeled the fourth alternative as Russian roulette because it is an odd combination of wanting a high risk in an environment that doesn't usually reward risk takers.

Organizational Culture Alternatives

	Reward	
	Avoid Punishment	*Positive Recognition*
Old Approaches	*Bureaucracy*	*Efficient*
(Low risk)	*(Routine/Procedures)*	*(Please the boss)*
Risk		
New Approaches	*Russian*	*Entrepreneurial*
(High Risk)	*roulette*	*(Innovative/Fun)*

Some of the readers of this book will have experienced several of the four business atmospheres described above. There is no one right answer for everyone!! The grid is just an attempt to analyze the mindset of the associate with the environment of their organization. "Peace-of-Mind" can best be expected when the associate is comfortable with the environment of his or her business unit.

Not every job permits a high degree of creativity and that's comfortable for people who enjoy and thrive in a structured environment. Associates who want innovation, high risk, positive recognition and a rapidly evolving atmosphere will naturally seek jobs in companies that provide that atmosphere.

The managers who choose to create an empowering environment will be most successful if:

1. they have the strong leadership and support of the head of the business unit to pursue this goal,

2. the leader or his/her successor continues the empowerment emphasis year after year, and

3. all parts of the business unit are respectful of the others and all encourage the same values.

The world is a looking glass and gives back to every man the reflection of his own face.

William Thackeray

Creative teams are not a panacea. But, they can open up new approaches to improving the competitiveness of a business.

35

Creative Teams

The alternative to bureaucratic, rigid organization structures is creative teams. Teams can be established for short projects or major undertakings. They are not just new names for the old "departments" in a bureaucracy.

Teams can have any number of people and last for any length of time. To be accepted by the organization, team membership must be voluntary. If a person doesn't want to be on a given team, don't force them. Over time, if the team produces useful results, the individual who opted out will have other chances to participate.

Expect almost everyone to have a lot of questions about teams. If it is new in an organization, people may consider a team as "a waste of time" or "something we can live without," or "something that keeps us from more important work."

After several teams enjoy success and recognition for a job well done, team membership becomes more attractive.

A key reason why teams have a difficult time at first is because people aren't prepared for a new paradigm. A team leader is not the supervisor or manager. Being a team leader requires a lot of persuasion and facilitation skills because the team leader doesn't have hiring and firing power or performance review power. Training is needed to educate everyone on the roles of team members and team leaders/facilitators, which are summarized below.

Team Member's Roles
Listen carefully to everyone's comments
Participate in discussion with creative and problem-solving ideas
Commit to group decisions

Team Leader/Facilitator Roles
Start and end meeting

Establish agenda

Manage conflict

Summarize ideas

Seek out multiple solutions

Seek outside resources as needed

Seek consensus

See that team decisions are made and implemented

If someone in the management of a business is ignoring the recommendations or actions of teams or ridiculing them, success of the concept is severely jeopardized. The support of teams is important by the CEO (Chief Empowerment Officer) as well as the other opinion leaders in the organization.

If a team isn't being productive, don't continue it. Trial and error should be expected. Remember that the goal is unleashing business creativity and that can happen from individuals as well as teams. The bigger the challenge, the more likely that a team will be needed.

Keep teams vibrant with new challenges. Don't have meetings just because it is 10:00 a.m. on Wednesday.

Associates need to get together periodically to solve problems or develop a new initiative. They should be encouraged to do so within or outside of the teams in effect at the time, if they want to.

Meetings should be as short as possible and involve only those key people needed to analyze a situation and proceed with a solution. Individual and group initiatives need to be encouraged. Any associate should be permitted to initiate a meeting; often meetings will not include a manager.

Periodically, teams should be reviewed, continued, modified in goals, or discontinued. Everyone in the organization should know who is participating on each team so they can contact someone to get their ideas included in the team's analysis. Teams that involve associates from different parts of the organization are often very useful in generating a broadly based consensus.

Creative teams are not a panacea. But, they can open up new approaches to improving the competitiveness of a business. They should be utilized with seriousness — not as a short-term experiment.

Without forgiveness life is governed by an endless cycle of resentment and retaliation.
Robert Assagioli

To assure that your candidates for corporate management positions are prepared for the scope of their responsibilities, you will want to consider a creative approach of management development like the ET (Experience and Training) model described.

36

A Creative Approach to Management Development

Career development requires a plan and creative thought. Does your company provide a comprehensive management development program that includes Experience and Training (ET) as important elements for all associates?

Goal: Prepare associates for satisfying careers and top management positions while helping the ABC organization grow profitably.

Discussion: An important part of the associates' education comes from the variety of business experiences they are exposed to in their ABC organization line management positions.

However, there is never enough time to rotate all of the good candidates to all parts of the company.

ET / EXPERIENCE + TRAINING

Fills the education gaps to assure that all candidates have a good basic appreciation of all the parts of business in addition to the areas where they have extensive line management experience.

ASSOCIATE: JOE FIELDER - Experience (E) and Training (T)

Professional Areas	Years of Experience (Years)	Level 101 0-2 Years	Level 201 3-5 Years	Level 301 6 Years+
Operations		T		
Marketing				
Sales				
Finance	E8			T
Human Resources				
Engineering				
Research		(T)		
Client Support	E2		(T)	
Public Affairs				
Legal				

With eight years of experience in finance (E8) and two years of experience in client support (E2), Joe is a candidate for the training experiences shown with a "T." Joe and his management agreed to proceed with the bracketed (T) training sessions this year.

ASSOCIATE: MARY NELSON - Experience (E) and Training (T)

Professional Areas	Years of Experience (Years)	Level 101 0-2 Years	Level 201 3-5 Years	Level 301 6 Years+
Operations	E6			T
Marketing	E2		(T)	
Sales		(T)		
Finance				
Human Resources				
Engineering		T		
Research				
Client Support				
Public Affairs				
Legal				

With six years of experience in operations (E6) and two years of experience in marketing (E2), Mary is a candidate for the training experiences shown with a "T." Mary and her management agreed to proceed with the bracketed (T) training sessions this year.

ASSOCIATE: FRED SMITH - Experience (E) and Training (T)

Executive Briefings	Introduction	Advanced
◆ Business Center Management	Completed 1997	Scheduled 2000
◆ Defining and Managing Core Competencies	Scheduled 1999	
◆ Competitive Strategy Development	Completed 1998	
◆ Portfolio Management		
◆ Mergers and Acquisitions	Scheduled 2001	
◆ Government Issues		
◆ Environmental Issues		
◆ Corporate Governance		

Fred is a vice president. The training sessions he has completed in the past two years and the ones he is scheduled for in the next three years are a key part of his management development program.

To assure that your candidates for corporate management positions are prepared for the scope of their responsibilities, you will want to consider a creative approach of management development like the ET (Experience and Training) model described.

Hold fast to dreams, for if dreams die, life is a broken winged bird that cannot fly.

Langston Hughes

The internal workings of a company or business are only important if they ultimately serve the client. The client has the votes with his dollars to continue or discontinue every business.

37

Business Principles for the New Millennium

The following pages provide a variety of thoughts on strategic management and implementation approaches. They are designed to stir your thinking in a different way than many of the other chapters that focused on conversations between people. Is your business ready for 2005?

A: PRIORITIES AND MINDSET

In your company, if 100 associates were asked the question, "What is the number one priority in this business?" what would the answers be? Before reading further, just note on a piece of paper what the most frequent and second most frequent answers would be in your judgment. Look again at your written responses.

People working in a plant might say "Top Quality," "Low Cost," or "Safety." People in an R&D organization might say "New Products." People in a sales organization might say "Sales Revenue." People in a financial role might say "Profits" or "Return on Assets."

Consider the answer that some might give — "Satisfying Client Needs and Wants." How many of the 100 people in your business would have given that answer to the question? Those who would have recognized that the internal workings of a company or business are only important if they ultimately serve the client. The client has the votes with his or her dollars to continue or discontinue every business.

This isn't just philosophy. If people have certain priorities in their minds, that is how they behave. If we want behavior that puts the client first, we need to have that priority clear in everyone's mind.

Consider the plant where a stranger can visit and ask a machine operator, "What is the number one priority in this business?," and get an answer like "There are a lot of important priorities, but number one has to be to keep the client happy. If he orders a product and we can't deliver because we have had production problems, he can buy some other product and we have lost him. Also, if we send him a product that doesn't do what it is supposed to, we have an unhappy client. If he doesn't buy from us, we don't have the money to pay our bills and grow for the future. My job is at stake. Client satisfaction has to be our number one priority."

Suppose 90 out of 100 people in your organization would give an answer something like that. Would you be pleased?

B: CREATIVE IMPLEMENTATION IS THE KEY TO GOOD BUSINESS STRATEGY

The accepted wisdom in retailing is "the three most

important decisions for success are location, location, location." In business strategy, we suggest, the three most important decisions for success are implementation, implementation, and implementation.

Creative implementation as your company in today's market does it is the starting point for a good business strategy. How are you selling now? What markets are you serving now? What products and services are you offering now? What do your competitors offer now?

Creative implementation as you might do it is a second step. You could enter a new market with an existing product. You could merge with another company and join resources. You could focus on another part of the world where competition is weaker. You could develop a new product not now offered in the market. The key is thinking through how various strategic alternatives could pay back financially and for the associates of your company. Only in investigating what the creative implementation could look like, can you be comfortable with a new business strategy.

Creative implementation of the chosen business strategy effectively is essential to its success. Careful attention to effective communications inside the business and to the outside world is critical. Major strategies take a lot of time, creative thinking, patience and courage to implement. Years are often involved.

C: THE ULTIMATE IN MARKET SEGMENTA-TION: SITUATION SELLING

Market segmentation has been extensively utilized by marketing professionals for many years. Successful product managers and market segment managers have planned their strategies for new products, distribution systems and pricing with careful attention to the segments they perceive to exist in the marketplace (based on market research, hunch or whatever).

Some clients want fast delivery, some want rock bottom price with slow delivery acceptable, some want special services, some want a predictable monthly expenditure pattern, some refuse to make any firm monthly commitments, some want a firm two-year agreement, some want a month-to-month arrangement.

Enter situation selling. Situation selling occurs every day in every market. Salespeople have their company's products and services described in their briefcase ready to listen to a prospect's needs and fill them with their company's offerings. But often the offerings don't match the clients' needs. The client values an option that the salesperson has difficulty selling because it isn't in the approved list of prices or policies in his briefcase. The sale can't be closed on that call. The salesperson calls his manager or appropriate marketing people. If and when approval for an exception to current policy is received, the client can be visited again and the sale can be completed (if a competitor hasn't already gotten the order).

How skilled are your salespeople in negotiating in these situations? How do they initially react to a client? "We can't do that." Have they learned to say they work for a flexible company, a special request could be feasible and then proceed to frame a discussion which leaves the client feeling that the salesperson has carefully listened to their needs?

How prepared are your marketing people for many exceptions to standard offerings? Are your approval procedures streamlined? Can you get back to the client with a customized proposal promptly? Are you prepared for the different billing and shipping needs of different clients?

We all know from marketplace experience that every client feels his or her particular needs are most important. Are we prepared to customize our offerings to meet his or her needs? If we aren't, will competitors capture our business?

Situation selling is a growing phenomenon. Salespeople can be trained to customize offerings to increase sales. Marketing organizations can change their thinking from market segments in general to the major individual clients within the major segments. It won't be easy, but some competitors will make the move. What could happen to your business if you do it first in your market? Or if you do it last?

D: THE STRATEGIC POWER OF A SALES FORCE

Implementation and strategy are very related. With a focus on the client, the competitors, the needs and wants of the marketplace, business strategy is distinctly molded by how a company chooses to interface with the clients and prospects.

A product or service in search of a market is frustratingly familiar to everyone in business management. We recognize the importance of defining the market and client needs and designing products and services to uniquely meet the client needs. A sales force that is in the market every day talking to clients and fighting competitive offerings for market share is a very valuable resource. They provide direct access to the clients to listen to clients' feedback and explain the company's offerings. This two-way dialog is key to business success.

The primary contact with the client is the salesperson. The profit center of every business is in the marketplace so the effective communications between a business' salespeople and its clients and prospects is a critical implementation step to business success.

We all have personally experienced the power of an effective salesperson — one who sincerely listens to our needs, probes to clarify our needs, tests his offerings as a way to meet our needs, and suggests a solution to our needs in a courteous way. We buy from effective salespeople and enjoy it.

Anyone who has tried to generate a successful business from a product or service without a sales force knows how difficult it is. Manufacturer's representatives, direct mail, telemarketing, distributors or a direct sales force - some route has to be found to get access to clients and develop the two-way communication.

An established sales force can be a very good conduit for defining new offerings for meeting market needs. Also, an established sales force can have strategic power by having access and relationships with clients to sell them new product and service offerings. A well trained sales force is a significant competitive strength.

E: MERGER AND ACQUISITION FACILITATOR

Mergers, acquisitions and joint ventures — all are subject to the same basic problems.

- Financial issues usually take the center stage, and then legal issues become important.
- So much time and energy is spent on financial and legal issues (often in an adversarial mode) that many key issues are not adequately addressed:
  1. Do the people like each other?
  2. Do the people have a common business vision?
  3. Has the joint vision been shared, understood and accepted?
  4. Is there a good emotional as well as business fit?
  5. Are the two cultures likely to mesh or clash?
  6. Once the joint vision is concluded to be acceptable to both parties, have the key implementation steps been accepted (staff, facilities, communications, timing, and so on)?

Suggestions

An experienced facilitator is a tremendous asset to assuring a successful business and motivated staff. The experienced facilitator can guide both parties to avoid win/lose situations and focus on the common vision and win/win implementation steps. It takes a thoughtful business leader to recognize that he can benefit by having impartial assistance from a facilitator who is not adversarial.

An experienced facilitator can help an organization think through whether it should even consider a merger, acquisition or joint venture. The facilitator can be useful before, after, or in any phase. It's like an insurance policy on the successful outcome of the transaction with special attention on the human emotional variables.

F: DEFINING STRATEGIC BUSINESSES

As the graphic on the next page shows, a careful analysis of a corporation is needed to establish good strategic business goals. Every corporation needs to carefully analyze its portfolio to identify its strong and weak business units.

DEFINING STRATEGIC BUSINESSES

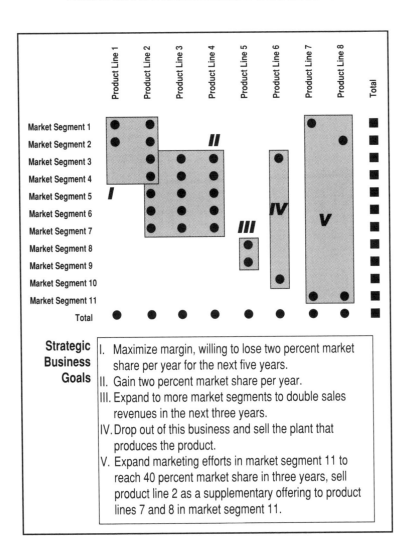

Strategic Business Goals

I. Maximize margin, willing to lose two percent market share per year for the next five years.
II. Gain two percent market share per year.
III. Expand to more market segments to double sales revenues in the next three years.
IV. Drop out of this business and sell the plant that produces the product.
V. Expand marketing efforts in market segment 11 to reach 40 percent market share in three years, sell product line 2 as a supplementary offering to product lines 7 and 8 in market segment 11.

G. TARGET MARKET SEGMENT

As the graphic below shows, there are 16 important decisions to penetrate each target market segment with your product or service. Defining target markets and the 16 important decisions to penetrate each specific market is challenging creative work.

H. EIGHT ROUTES TO IMPROVED PROFITABILITY

(Two of the eight approaches should be the primary routes— all eight cannot successfully be emphasized simultaneously).

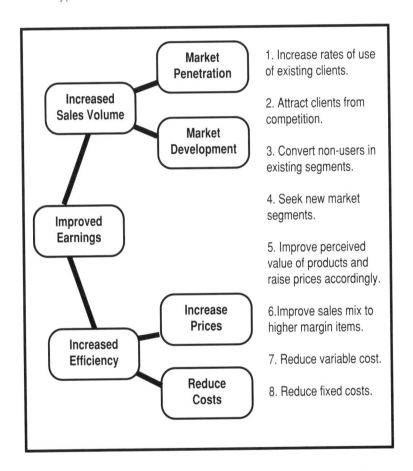

Love is life, and if you miss love, you miss life.
Leo Buscaglia

A satisfying career is achieved by gradually obtaining skills which help us to meet the challenges of increasing responsibility.

38

Training

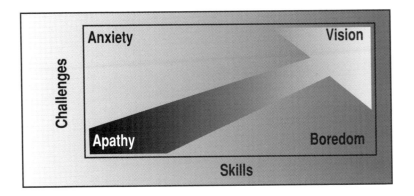

If we have many skills and our work provides very few challenges, we are in the boredom sector of the chart.

If we have very few skills and our work is very challenging, we are in the anxiety sector and training appears attractive to us to obtain new skills for our personal growth.

A satisfying career is achieved by gradually obtaining skills that help us to meet the challenges of increasing responsibility. Hence, personal growth and career growth go together and training is important every year along the way.

Training, formal and informal, is a method for renewal. All training takes a person through four stages.

Unconsciously Incompetent

When we enter a new area, we don't know what we don't know. We are novices or beginners.

Consciously Incompetent

The initial phases of training help us to gradually learn what it is we need to know to perform some position or responsibility.

Consciously Competent

After extensive training, we are quite competent in the new field. However, we have to still be very conscious of the necessary steps — first I do A, then B, then C.

Unconsciously Competent

This is the ultimate goal of training, but it requires a lot of individual practice so that the lessons learned become second nature.

Some examples might be:

1. The secretary who types 80 or more words per minute without looking at the keyboard or the computer screen and makes very few mistakes (training plus a lot of practice), or

2. the golfer who has a smooth, grooved swing and doesn't have to think about each step in the swing (training plus a lot of practice...professionals hit 1,000 balls a day), or

3. the manager who naturally compliments the members of her organization on their good work ten times as much as she corrects them for mistakes (training plus a lot of practice in empowering associates so it is second nature and is done naturally and consistently).

Formal training programs can only be expected to help the students reach the level of being consciously competent. Extensive individual practice is necessary to reach the goal of unconsciously competent. This is true for bus drivers, lawyers, mechanics, painters, managers, salespeople, and so on.

Once we have the desire for personal growth, training is very valuable. Experience and Training (ET) were described in chapter 36. Both are necessary for personal growth.

Courage is the price that life exacts for granting peace.

Amelia Earhart

We are each unique and, therefore, we need to reflect on how best to utilize our uniqueness. There is no question we have it, the only question is what we choose to do with it.

39

Influencing Your Destiny

The Uniqueness of You. We all have unique fingerprints. In addition to being physically unique, we are mentally unique, with different experiences in our brain's memory. With uniqueness of body, brain and experiences, certainly we each have different pasts, presents and futures. There are just no two identical human beings. Sure, we have a lot in common with our family, friends and co-workers in a business. But the exciting thought is we are each unique and, therefore, we need to reflect on how best to utilize our uniqueness. There is no question we have it, the only question is what we choose to do with it. Others can help, but we need to direct our own unique destiny. If we don't, who else can or will?

A Strategic Plan. To influence your personal destiny, a strategic plan is extremely useful. That must include a careful analysis of your personal strengths and weaknesses. Focus on the strengths. It isn't necessary for the world's best pole vaulter to even know how to swim. To develop a sound strategic plan, you will also have to assess the strengths and weaknesses of your competition. Strategically don't define your competition too narrowly. Is it really a requirement for the job you aspire to, for the winner to have a certain educational background, certain training and variety of experiences? Now, survey the areas of opportunity (the markets). How do you and your competitors match up to the needs of a given market, or group of jobs? Understanding yourself, your competition and the market needs are critical steps to a good personal strategic plan for influencing your destiny. Now comes the critical part.

The Positioning of You. As a unique individual, you deserve a unique position in the marketplace of business opportunity. We all tend to enjoy most what we do well. Few people like to make themselves unhappy, by forcing themselves to do something they don't do well. It's natural to seek an area of psychological comfort. So the positioning of you is your unique task. You, and only you, can decide what position best suits your unique set of talents compared to the market needs. Pick a field that you can be comfortable with for a number of years. Once you have pinpointed the field and possible position, picture it in your mind, write about it on paper, live it and it will be yours. Once you have committed yourself to that position, it will radiate from you to the world. Your actions and words will help you strengthen your hold on your position in the market. The positioning of you as an individual is influencing your own destiny.

Is It Worth It? Consider the alternatives. Others decide what's best for you. Others tell you about your strengths and weaknesses. Others think through alternatives for you. Only you really know what destiny you want and with careful analysis, preparation and dedication, you can achieve it. Sure, it's worth it! To sit back and let the world, your parents, your manager, your teacher or your coach influence your life is fine; we all need input. But the important positioning decisions are up to you; it's your destiny.

Self-Fulfilling Prophesies. Think about yourself as a loser and you will be one. Think about your business as over the hill and it will be. Think about your loss in market share and you will lose some more. Think about opportunities rather than problems and you are on the road to effective business management. Think about your strengths and your company's strengths and you will grow personally and corporately toward your goals. Learn lessons from the past but don't dwell on them — focus on the future. After all, you can only live this moment and into the future.

Most people are about as happy as they make up their minds to be.
Abraham Lincoln

We cannot change our past...we cannot change the inevitable. The only thing we can do is play on the one string we have, and that is our attitude.

40

The Learning Corporation

Time is our friend and time is our enemy.

In a rapidly moving marketplace, the Learning Corporation is one that has mastered the ability to make time its friend. A normal cycle may be:

The Learning Cycle

Develop a concept for a new product or service.	Compare concept to products and services now on the market.	Develop first prototype.	Test in the market with clients.

→

Produce final prototype.	Test in the market with clients.	Develop implementation steps for scale-up.	Plan for a scaled-up introduction.

←

Compare with competition for cost, selling price, and commercial viability.	Launch in U.S.	Decide on international use of product or service.

→

Each step takes time. From conceiving a new product or service to launching it successfully commercially can be a three month to three year process. Growing the business to a national or international level can be another five to ten year process. The Learning Corporation finds ways to cut down on these long time periods.

First, the Learning Corporation needs to be a corporation with an attitude. The jargon in today's society "having an attitude" needs to be modified a bit in a corporation but the concept of an attitude is what is definitely needed. A famous verse on attitude is:

ATTITUDE

"The longer I live, the more I realize the impact of attitude on life. Attitude, to me, is more important than facts. It is more important than the past, than education, than money, than circumstances, than failures, than successes, than what other people think or say or do. It is more important than appearance, giftedness, or skill. It will make or break a company...a church...a home. The remarkable thing is we each have a choice every day regarding the attitude we will embrace for that day. We cannot change our past...we cannot change the inevitable. The only thing we can do is play on the one string we have, and that is our attitude. I am convinced that life is 10 percent of what happens to me and 90 percent how I react to it. And so it is with you...we are in charge of our Attitudes.

-- Charles Swindoll

The attitude the Learning Corporation needs is:

♦ Believe that the best way to meet the needs of a client is to first find out his needs. (So many unsuccessful product and service solutions go to market looking for a problem that doesn't exist or exists at a very small scale.)

- Accept that the clients are our best teachers. (Show them a prototype and they will help you modify it. Experiment, cut and try. Get constant feedback from clients; how better can you be sure the product or service will commercially meet real needs?)
- Do everything in hours, days and weeks not months, years and decades. (Time is a friend for those who move fast.)
- Avoid bureaucracy. (Everyone must be either serving a client or directly helping someone who is; layers and layers of paper shuffling and internal checks and double checks slows things down and inhibits creative problem solving.)
- Encourage everyone in the corporation to feel free to talk to anyone they choose at any time to help them solve their problem or reach their goal. (Protecting turf and checking through your manager stifles individual initiative. People want responsibility, authority and freedom.)
- Let anyone call an impromptu meeting anytime. (We all know that hallway conversations are often more productive than two-hour meetings; so encourage more three to ten minute meetings of people who can help each other with a goal.)
- Consider everyone in the Learning Corporation as an associate — not an employee, an hourly worker, a salaried worker, a manager, a boss (boss spelled backwards is double SOB). The attitude of everyone as an associate is critical.

Beyond those attitudes, one more is extremely critical: cut

down the time lags by buying outside knowledge when you need it. Forget about not invented here; if the knowledge needed is technical, consider licensing someone else's patent or technology. If the knowledge needed is market knowledge, find a way to purchase a lot of knowledgeable clients to add to your market knowledge base. If you need computerization knowledge, get it from someone on the cutting edge not someone who is way behind the times.

The Learning Corporation needs an attitude. The attitude needs to be - don't expect to invent everything yourself. Time is your friend if you can reach a commercial stage rapidly. Those who remain in ivory tower research for years may invent excellent products and services for use in ivory towers. But the real world requires product and service research and development to be in the hurly burly of the marketplace - where the clients are, where the problems are and where the solutions are for the creative observer. Empowering the clients by involving them is a sound business practice.

The alternative to not being a Learning Corporation: not financially attractive and not as much fun to work in.

The only true happiness comes from squandering ourselves for a good purpose.
William Cooper

The Chief Executive Officer (CEO) must also be the Chief Empowerment Officer (CEO) if a business is going to evolve to "Unleashing business creativity...to empower your clients."

41

The Corporate Culture

What makes a company very desirable as a place to work? Is it past business success, excellent products and services, management leadership, or what?

First of all, a company that is attractive as a place to work to many people isn't attractive to others. Some people have a value system that they feel is not compatible with working for a tobacco company, a defense contractor, a government agency or a bank.

For the most part, people work for a company because they feel the company offers:

a. interesting work,

b. fair compensation, and

c. a pleasant working and learning atmosphere.

There is a high emotional impact from the way that associates are treated. Positive reinforcement is greatly appreciated. Recognition and praise are very important to help people motivate themselves.

Negative reinforcement is very common in the form of criticism and threats in some companies and is not well received emotionally by associates.

Psychologists have found in their studies that people are much more likely to respond constructively for a company in an atmosphere of positive reinforcement than they are in a negative reinforcement atmosphere.

In my line management and consulting experiences, 16 dimensions of corporate culture help reveal the essence of the corporate culture. I have found it possible to have a group discuss their perceptions and attitudes on these 16 dimensions and then document their view of the present company culture on one single page. We call it "Working at ABC Corporation" and use it for recruiting new associates as well as refreshing our present staff on our core beliefs.

Dimensions of a One-Page "Culture Statement"

* Clients/Customers   * Pride   * Teamwork
* Leadership   * Responsibility   * Personal Initiative
* Recognition   * Celebration   * Associates/Employees
* Entrepreneurial Spirit   * Bureaucracy   * Job Descriptions
* Organization Chart   * Compensation   * Renewal
* Professional Attitude

As an example of how the 16 point analysis is done, several members of the organization select ratings from 1 to 10 on each of the categories, such as Teamwork, from the following table:

1 — Teamwork is not noticeable. Everybody and every organization is out for themselves.

4 — Team effort is sometimes utilized. Generally, departments work separately.

7 — Team effort is frequently observed. Management encourages teamwork, but some associates focus on what they feel is best for their department.

10— Teamwork is always in effect. There are no turf battles. Full cooperation is expected by management and all other associates to empower the clients.

They rate Teamwork Now - (say 4), and Teamwork Goal - (say 8). 8 was selected because the reasonable goal was felt to be between 7 and 10, closer to 7.

This process is done by a diverse group on all 16 dimensions and is a very revealing exercise to all involved.

If the corporate culture that exists is the one that is desired for the competitive health of the business, all that is needed is consistent communication and celebration of the basic principles throughout the organization. If changes are desired, this 16 point analysis will usually pinpoint the areas needing change.

In any case, the final one-page summary must be consistent with everyday actions in the company. Actions speak much louder than words and if the actions aren't following the Culture Statement, then the Culture Statement isn't accomplishing its purpose to help mold the atmosphere in the business. The Chief Empowerment Officer (CEO) must monitor the organization and lead it in the necessary direction for the long-term success of the business.

The Chief Executive Officer (CEO) must also be the

Chief Empowerment Officer (CEO) if a business is going to evolve to "Unleashing business creativity…to empower your clients."

Leadership must be clear and consistent for an organization to believe that the value system of the CEO is expected to be the value system of everyone else in the organization. The Chief Empowerment Officer leads effectively when all the associates in the organization are empowered to empower the clients. The ultimate power, as it should be, resides with the clients.

To be what we are, and to become what we are capable of becoming, is the only end of life.

Robert Louis Stevenson

Appendix

42

Order form for more copies of
Unleashing Business Creativity

TO: Bill Peter & Associates

   6650 Vernon Hills Road

   Edina, MN 55436

FROM:

Name_____

Address _____

City, State, Zip _____

Home Phone:_____

Work Phone:_____

Please mail your order to the address above along with your personal check.

Order authorized by:_____

                             Your signature

                _____

                             Order Date

____ Copies of *Unleashing Business Creativity* at $6.00 per copy = $_____

(60 percent discount from $14.95 price - minimum order of 24 copies)

Shipping and Handling

(Allow 2-3 weeks for delivery - $10.00 per case of 24 copies)   = $_____

Total Cost (Your Personal Check Enclosed)   = $_____

For more information call toll free at 1-877- 466-6846

43

About the Author

Bill Peter is a management consultant, realtor and author whose home is in a suburb of Minneapolis, Minnesota. Bill is dedicated to unleashing his own and others' creativity in many business environments.

He has managed businesses and been a management consultant to many diverse companies around the world: computer software, electronics, real estate, industrial chemicals, textiles, retail pharmacy, health care, automobiles, tires, appliances, education, advertising, medical products, art products, church development and community development.

Bill also wrote a clients' guide to the financial and emotional aspects of buying or selling a home in his book *I'M MOVING - Eliminating the anxiety of buying or selling a home* (published August 1998 by Beaver's Pond Press, Inc.).

The "Peace-of-Mind" series by Bill Peter includes Book One (*I'M MOVING*) and Book Two (*Unleashing Business Creativity*). This series focuses on the big events or issues in everyone's life (one's home in Book One, and one's work in Book Two). In late 1999, Bill Peter is planning to publish Book Three in the "Peace of Mind" series entitled *As the Soul Teaches*.

For additional information online: www.billpeter.com